SPRING FEVER BEGINS!

*I*n the spirit of rejuvenation that spring brings, Kraft Foods has compiled this creative collection of simple and delicious menus filled with appetizers, main dishes, side dishes, salads, desserts and beverages that are ideal for all of your springtime events. Made with ingredients from the *Family of Fine Food Products of Kraft Foods* and tested in our own Kraft Creative Kitchens, each recipe combines ease, style and great taste to bring refreshing results to your table. And to help you set the stage for the season's festivities—from casual get-togethers to delightful holiday celebrations—we've put together an entire chapter on how to thoughtfully dress your table for the occasion.

We've also sprinkled several tips throughout the book for selecting, storing and preparing spring's best produce. After winter, the fresh, brightly colored fruits and vegetables of the season are a welcome sight.

All of us at Kraft Foods hope you'll find this *Springtime Celebrations* book full of the inspiration of the new season.

EDITOR	*Mary Jo Plutt*
ART DIRECTOR	*Brian Shearer*
RECIPE DEVELOPMENT	*Kraft Creative Kitchens*
PHOTOGRAPHY	*Tom Firak*
	Jose Pascual
	Joe Polivka
FOOD STYLING	*Amy Andrews*
	Irene Bertolucci
	Bonnie Rabert
PROP STYLING	*Bonnie Kaplan*
	Cindy Neberz

CONTENTS

SPRINGTIME MENUS 5

*Having family and friends over to celebrate spring is a breeze
with this selection of menus and recipes.*

DRESSING YOUR TABLE 89

*Make your springtime table look as sensational as the food it
holds with these simple, yet distinctive decorating ideas.*

Printed in Hong Kong. Produced by Meredith Custom Publishing,
1912 Grand Ave., Des Moines, Iowa 50309-3379.

*Pictured on front cover (clockwise from upper left): Sour Cream Pound Cake (recipe, page 77), Pineapple Banana
Coconut Cream Pie (recipe, page 19), **PHILLY** Cream Cheese Classic Cheesecake (recipe, page 62).*

SPRINGTIME MENUS

From fun and frivolous to refined and regal, here are 20 great menus that rejoice in the season. Whether it's the Kentucky Derby, Easter or Cinco de Mayo, or just an opportunity to enjoy a relaxing meal on your porch with neighbors or video night with family members, you'll find the right foods here to set the mood and delight your guests.

Clockwise from top left:
Sugar and Spice Coffee (recipe, page 7), Coffee Chocolate Chunk Cookies (recipe, page 7), White Chocolate Mousse Banana Tart (recipe, page 8), Sunshine Punch (recipe, page 9), Chocolate Dipped Delights (recipe, page 6)

Spring Celebration Dessert Party

There's no sweeter way to ring in spring than with this tempting array of delightful desserts and nibbles! All the treats here can be made in advance, giving you plenty of time to visit with your guests.

White Chocolate Mousse Banana Tart

Cute and Cuddly Bunny Cake

Coffee Chocolate Chunk Cookies

Chocolate Dipped Delights

Caramel Balls

Sugar and Spice Coffee

Sunshine Punch

Chocolate Dipped Delights

Melt, dip and dig in! That's all there is to this medley of chocolate-dipped fruit, cookies and pretzels (photo, pages 4–5).

Prep time: 10 minutes plus standing
Microwave time: 2 minutes

1 package (4 ounces) BAKER'S GERMAN'S Sweet Chocolate *or* 1 package (8 squares) BAKER'S Semi-Sweet Chocolate *or* 1 package (6 squares) BAKER'S Premium White Chocolate

Whole strawberries, dried apricots, orange slices, star fruit, chocolate sandwich cookies *or* pretzels

MICROWAVE chocolate in microwavable bowl on HIGH 2 minutes or until chocolate is almost melted, stirring halfway through heating time. Stir until chocolate is completely melted.

DIP fruit, cookies or pretzels into chocolate; let excess chocolate drip off. Let stand or refrigerate on wax paper-lined tray 30 minutes or until chocolate is firm. Drizzle with additional melted chocolate, if desired.

Makes about 2 dozen.

Note: For double-dipped fruit, cookies or pretzels, first dip in melted white chocolate; let stand to dry. Then dip in melted semi-sweet chocolate.

FLAVORED COFFEES

*Liqueurs, chocolate or brown sugar and cinnamon turn
a plain cup of java into a taste celebration.*

CAFE DIABLO (photo, page 45): Stir 1½ ounces (3 tablespoons) brandy and ¾ ounce (1½ tablespoons) coffee-flavored liqueur into 6 ounces hot prepared instant *or* brewed MAXWELL HOUSE *or* YUBAN Coffee in a mug. Garnish with thawed COOL WHIP Whipped Topping *or* whipped cream, if desired.

COFFEE CHOCOLATÉ: Stir 1 tablespoon chocolate-flavored syrup *or* KRAFT Hot Fudge Topping into 6 ounces hot prepared instant *or* brewed MAXWELL HOUSE *or* YUBAN Coffee in a mug. Garnish with thawed COOL WHIP Whipped Topping *or* whipped cream and sprinkle with ground cinnamon.

SUGAR AND SPICE COFFEE (photo, pages 4–5): Stir 1 teaspoon brown sugar into 6 ounces hot prepared instant *or* brewed MAXWELL HOUSE *or* YUBAN Coffee in a mug. Serve with a cinnamon stick.

Brewing Tip:

SPICED COFFEE: When brewing ground MAXWELL HOUSE *or* YUBAN Coffee, sprinkle ½ to 1 teaspoon ground cinnamon over each ½ cup coffee grounds used.

COFFEE CHOCOLATE CHUNK COOKIES

*Make these gourmet cookies with either regular or decaffeinated brewed coffee.
Either choice will result in a delicious, rich coffee flavor (photo, pages 4–5).*

Prep time: 10 minutes
*Baking time per cookie sheet: 12 minutes
   plus cooling*

1¾ cups flour
¼ teaspoon baking soda
¾ cup (1½ sticks) butter *or* margarine
¾ cup granulated sugar
½ cup firmly packed brown sugar
¼ cup chilled freshly brewed strong MAXWELL HOUSE Coffee
1 egg
1 teaspoon vanilla
1 package (8 squares) BAKER'S Semi-Sweet Chocolate, cut into chunks
1½ cups chopped walnuts

MIX flour and baking soda in small bowl. Beat butter in large bowl with electric mixer on medium speed to soften. Gradually add sugars, beating until light and fluffy. Beat in coffee, egg and vanilla. Gradually add flour mixture, beating well after each addition. Stir in chocolate and chopped walnuts.

DROP dough by rounded teaspoonfuls 2 inches apart on cookie sheet.

BAKE in preheated 375°F oven for 10 to 12 minutes or until golden brown. Remove from cookie sheet. Cool on wire rack.

Makes 5 dozen.

CARAMEL BALLS

For an eye-catching touch, place these delightfully chewy balls in paper candy cups to serve or present as gifts.

Prep time: 15 minutes
Microwave time:
2 minutes OR
Top of stove cooking
time: 10 minutes

20 caramels
1 tablespoon water
2 cups POST HONEY BUNCHES OF OATS Cereal, any variety, divided

MICROWAVE caramels and water in medium microwavable bowl on HIGH 1½ to 2 minutes or until caramels are melted and mixture is smooth, stirring every minute.

STIR in 1½ cups of the cereal. Mix lightly until well coated. With hands slightly moistened with cold water, form into 1-inch balls. Crush remaining ½ cup cereal; roll balls in crushed cereal to coat.

Makes about 20.

TOP OF STOVE: Melt caramels with water in heavy saucepan on low heat, stirring frequently until smooth. Continue as directed.

WHITE CHOCOLATE MOUSSE BANANA TART

Your guests will go bananas over this luscious pie—it's a quick concoction of fresh banana slices and an easy white-chocolate mousse mixture that's crowned with drizzled, melted semi-sweet chocolate (photo, pages 4–5).

Prep time: 15 minutes plus cooling
and refrigerating
Microwave time: 2 minutes

1 refrigerated pie crust (9 inches)
1 package (6 squares) BAKER'S Premium White Chocolate
1½ cups heavy *or* whipping cream, divided
2 bananas, sliced
1 square BAKER'S Semi-Sweet Chocolate, melted

PREPARE and bake pie crust as directed on package for unfilled 1-crust pie using 9-inch tart pan with removable bottom or 9-inch pie plate.

MICROWAVE white chocolate and ¼ cup of the cream in large microwavable bowl on HIGH 2 minutes or until white chocolate is almost melted, stirring halfway through heating time. Stir until white chocolate is completely melted. Cool 20 minutes or to room temperature, stirring occasionally.

BEAT remaining 1¼ cups cream in chilled medium bowl with electric mixer on medium speed until soft peaks form. DO NOT OVERBEAT. Fold ½ of the whipped cream into white chocolate mixture. Fold in remaining whipped cream just until blended.

LINE pie crust with banana slices. Spoon mousse mixture over banana slices. Drizzle with melted chocolate. Refrigerate 1 hour or until ready to serve. Remove from tart pan before serving.

Makes 8 servings.

CUTE AND CUDDLY BUNNY CAKE

*Celebrate Easter with this tasty charmer that will please every
egg-hunter in your house and garden.*

Prep time: 20 minutes

3¼ cups BAKER'S ANGEL FLAKE Coconut, divided
  Yellow and red food colorings
 2 baked 9-inch round cake layers, cooled
 1 tub (8 ounces) COOL WHIP Whipped Topping, thawed
  Assorted candies for garnish

TINT 1 cup of the coconut yellow using yellow
food coloring. Tint ¼ cup of the coconut pink
using red food coloring.

LEAVE 1 cake layer whole; cut remaining cake
layer as shown in illustration below. Using a
small amount of whipped topping to hold pieces
together, arrange cake on serving tray as shown
in illustration.

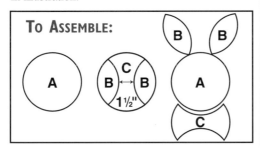

FROST cake with remaining whipped topping.
Sprinkle bunny's cheeks and center of ears with
pink coconut. Sprinkle remaining 2 cups white
coconut over bunny's head and outer edges of
ears. Sprinkle bunny's bow tie with yellow
coconut. Decorate face and bow tie with candies.
Store cake in refrigerator.

Makes 12 to 16 servings.

SUNSHINE PUNCH

*Brighten those rainy spring afternoons with a pitcher of this
fruity thirst quencher (photo, pages 4–5).*

Prep time: 10 minutes plus refrigerating

 1 envelope KOOL-AID Tropical Punch Flavor Sugar Free
   Low Calorie Soft Drink Mix
 6 cups cold water and ice cubes
 2 cups chilled orange juice

PLACE soft drink mix in large plastic or glass
pitcher. Add water and ice cubes; stir to dissolve.

STIR in orange juice. Refrigerate until ready to
serve.

Makes 8 (1 cup) servings.

May Day Breakfast

April showers bring May flowers—and a good reason to celebrate the first day of May. Do it in style with the ease and colorful flair of this delicious menu.

Confetti Fruit Cups

Bacon Breakfast Casserole

Crumble Top Banana Muffins

Blueberry Sour Cream Coffee Cake

Russian Tea (recipe, page 61)

Confetti Fruit Cups

When you know you'll be pressed for time, cut up the fruit and mix it with the prepared TANG the night before. Then, in the morning, just top the fruit and serve.

Prep time: 15 minutes plus refrigerating

1½ cups prepared TANG Brand Orange Flavor Drink Mix
6 cups sliced *or* diced fresh fruit
2 tablespoons TANG Brand Orange Flavor Drink Mix
1 container (8 ounces) BREYERS *or* KNUDSEN Vanilla Lowfat Yogurt

Mix prepared TANG and fruit in large bowl; toss to coat well. Cover and refrigerate.

Stir 2 tablespoons dry TANG into yogurt until well blended in a small bowl. Cover and refrigerate.

Serve fruit in small melon shells, if desired, or spoon into individual dishes. Top each serving with yogurt mixture.

Makes 12 servings.

Clockwise from top left: Crumble Top Banana Muffins (recipe, page 12), Russian Tea (recipe, page 61), Bacon Breakfast Casserole (recipe, page 12), Confetti Fruit Cups

BACON BREAKFAST CASSEROLE

*Here's a great make-ahead entrée for an early
morning brunch (photo, page 10).*

Prep time: 20 minutes plus refrigerating
Baking time: 1 hour plus standing

  8 slices white bread, crusts trimmed, cut in half
 12 slices OSCAR MAYER Center Cut Bacon, crisply cooked,
     crumbled
  1 can (4 ounces) sliced mushrooms, drained
  2 green onions, sliced
 1½ cups (6 ounces) KRAFT Natural Shredded Mild Cheddar
     Cheese
  4 eggs, beaten
  2 cups milk

PLACE 8 bread-slice halves on bottom of greased
8-inch square baking pan. Sprinkle bacon,
mushrooms, onions and cheese on bread. Cover
with remaining 8 bread-slice halves.

MIX eggs and milk; pour over bread. Cover.
Refrigerate 1 hour or overnight.

BAKE, uncovered, at 350°F for 1 hour. Let stand
10 minutes before serving.

Makes 6 servings.

CRUMBLE TOP BANANA MUFFINS

*POST BANANA NUT CRUNCH Cereal makes a no-fuss crumble
topping for these moist muffins (photo, page 10).*

Prep time: 15 minutes
Baking time: 20 minutes

 1¼ cups flour
  1 tablespoon CALUMET Baking Powder
  ⅛ teaspoon salt
  1 egg *or* 2 egg whites
  ½ cup skim milk
  ⅓ cup firmly packed brown sugar
  3 tablespoons oil
 1½ cups POST BANANA NUT CRUNCH Cereal
  1 cup finely chopped bananas

CRUMBLE TOPPING:
  ½ cup POST BANANA NUT CRUNCH Cereal, slightly
     crushed
  1 tablespoon brown sugar
  ½ teaspoon ground cinnamon
  1 teaspoon oil

MIX flour, baking powder and salt in large bowl.
Beat eggs in small bowl; stir in milk, ⅓ cup
brown sugar and 3 tablespoons oil. Add to flour
mixture; stir just until moistened. (Batter will be
lumpy.) Stir in 1½ cups cereal and bananas.

SPOON batter into greased or paper-lined muffin
pan, filling each cup ⅔ full. To make crumble
topping: Mix ½ cup slightly crushed cereal,
1 tablespoon brown sugar and cinnamon. Drizzle
with 1 teaspoon oil; stir until crumbly. Sprinkle
evenly over muffins.

BAKE in preheated 400°F oven for 20 minutes
or until lightly browned. Serve warm.

Makes 12.

Blueberry Sour Cream Coffee Cake

*Enjoy the layers of rich cake and crunchy blueberry cereal
in this tempting morning treat.*

Prep time: 20 minutes
Baking time: 40 minutes

  2 cups POST BLUEBERRY MORNING Cereal, slightly
      crushed
  1 teaspoon ground cinnamon
  2 tablespoons butter *or* margarine, melted
  2 cups flour
  1 teaspoon baking soda
  ½ teaspoon *each* CALUMET Baking Powder *and* salt
  ½ cup (1 stick) butter *or* margarine
  1 cup sugar
  2 eggs
  ½ teaspoon vanilla
  1 cup BREAKSTONE'S *or* KNUDSEN Sour Cream

Mix cereal, cinnamon and 2 tablespoons
melted butter in small bowl; set aside. Mix flour,
baking soda, baking powder and salt in another
small bowl.

Beat ½ cup butter in large bowl with electric
mixer on medium speed to soften. Gradually add
sugar, beating until light and fluffy. Add eggs,
1 at a time, beating well after each addition. Stir
in vanilla.

Add flour mixture alternately with sour cream,
beating after each addition until smooth. Pour
½ of the batter into greased 9-inch square pan;
top with ½ of the cereal mixture. Repeat layers.

Bake in preheated 350°F oven for 40 minutes
or until toothpick inserted in center comes out
clean. Serve warm. Cut into squares.

Makes 12 servings.

Best of Spring

Melons

There are many kinds of melons—from the conventional cantaloupe to the more exotic and
fragrant galia. In general, melons are large, oval or round fruits that have thick rinds and soft,
juicy, honey-sweet flesh.

Though thumping melons in the produce section may be fun, it doesn't necessarily tell you much
about freshness. Depending on the variety, you should look for certain specific characteristics
when selecting a fresh melon. Some characteristics are universal: Melons should feel heavy for
their size and be well shaped. Bypass those with skin that is wet, dented, bruised or cracked.

ℬABY SHOWER LUNCHEON

Mark the impending arrival of a new baby with this special midday menu. Dainty finger foods served alongside an elegant, but quick, main-dish salad are certain to impress the mother-to-be and guests.

PHILLY Cream Cheese Cucumber Dill Dip
with assorted crudités

Cheddar and Onion Bites

Chicken Chutney Salad

Easy Carrot Cake

Fudge Balls

MAXWELL HOUSE *or* **YUBAN** Coffee

CHICKEN CHUTNEY SALAD

Chutney is a flavorful condiment that typically contains fruit, vinegar, sugar and spices. Look for it at your grocery store alongside other condiments such as pickles, jams, jellies or vinegars.

Prep time: 15 minutes plus refrigerating

- ¾ cup MIRACLE WHIP Salad Dressing
- ¼ cup mango chutney
- 4 cups cubed cooked chicken
- 1 cup chopped peeled jicama
- 1 cup halved red grapes
- ½ cup sliced celery
  Salt *and* pepper
- ½ cup coarsely chopped pecans, toasted
- 8 slices OSCAR MAYER Center Cut Bacon, crisply cooked, crumbled

MIX salad dressing and chutney until well blended.

ADD chicken, jicama, grapes and celery; mix lightly. Season to taste with salt and pepper. Refrigerate.

SPRINKLE with pecans and bacon just before serving; mix lightly.

Makes 6 main-dish servings.

Easy Carrot Cake (recipe, page 17)
Chicken Chutney Salad

CHEDDAR AND ONION BITES

One taste of these melted morsels will keep your guests coming back for more!

Prep time: 10 minutes
Broiling time: 3 minutes

- ⅓ cup KRAFT Real Mayonnaise
- 2 tablespoons chopped green onion
- 16 slices cocktail rye bread, toasted
- 1 package (10 ounces) CRACKER BARREL Sharp Natural Cheddar Cheese, thinly sliced

MIX mayonnaise and onion.

SPREAD on toasted bread slices. Top with cheese. Place on cookie sheet.

BROIL 2 to 3 minutes or until cheese is melted.

Makes 16.

PHILLY CREAM CHEESE CUCUMBER DILL DIP

What's the best way to seed a cucumber? Simply halve it lengthwise and scrape out the seeds with a small spoon.

Prep time: 10 minutes plus refrigerating

- 1 package (8 ounces) PHILADELPHIA BRAND Cream Cheese, softened
- ½ cup KRAFT Ranch Dressing
- 2 tablespoons milk
- 1 medium cucumber, peeled, seeded and chopped
- 2 tablespoons finely chopped onion
- 1 teaspoon dill weed
- ¼ teaspoon salt

MIX cream cheese, dressing and milk with electric mixer on medium speed until well blended.

STIR in remaining ingredients. Refrigerate.

SERVE with assorted cut-up vegetables.

Makes 3 cups.

VARIATION: Substitute PHILADELPHIA BRAND Neufchatel Cheese, ⅓ Less Fat than Cream Cheese, *or* PHILADELPHIA BRAND Soft Cream Cheese for regular cream cheese.

EASY CARROT CAKE

There's a secret KRAFT ingredient that adds a delicate moistness to this trouble-free winner. Skeptical? Try one bite, and you'll become a believer (photo, page 14).

Prep time: 25 minutes
Baking time: 35 minutes plus cooling

1¼ cups MIRACLE WHIP Salad Dressing

1 package (2-layer size) yellow cake mix

4 eggs

¼ cup water

2 teaspoons ground cinnamon

2 cups finely shredded carrots

½ cup chopped walnuts

1 package (8 ounces) PHILADELPHIA BRAND Cream Cheese, softened

1 tablespoon vanilla

3 to 3½ cups sifted powdered sugar

BEAT salad dressing, cake mix, eggs, water and cinnamon with electric mixer on medium speed until well blended. Stir in carrots and walnuts. Pour into greased 13x9-inch baking pan.

BAKE in preheated 350°F oven for 30 to 35 minutes or until toothpick inserted in center comes out clean. Cool completely.

BEAT cream cheese and vanilla with electric mixer on medium speed until well blended. Gradually add sugar, beating well after each addition. Frost cake.

Makes 10 to 12 servings.

FUDGE BALLS

Make these simple coffee-flavored fudge balls in your microwave oven.

Prep time: 10 minutes plus refrigerating
Microwave time: 2 minutes

1 package (8 squares) BAKER'S Semi-Sweet Chocolate

⅓ cup sweetened condensed milk

¼ cup freshly brewed MAXWELL HOUSE *or* YUBAN Coffee

½ cup chopped nuts

1 teaspoon vanilla

Suggested coatings: MAXWELL HOUSE *or* YUBAN Instant Coffee, unsweetened cocoa, ground nuts, graham cracker crumbs, cookie crumbs, BAKER'S ANGEL FLAKE Coconut, toasted

MICROWAVE chocolate, milk and coffee in large microwavable bowl on HIGH 2 minutes or until chocolate is almost melted, stirring halfway through heating time. Stir until chocolate is completely melted.

STIR in nuts and vanilla. Spread into 8-inch square pan. Refrigerate 2 hours or until firm enough to handle.

SHAPE into 1-inch balls. Roll in desired coatings. Store in refrigerator.

Makes about 2 dozen.

CINCO DE MAYO CELEBRATION

May 5th means fiesta time—and not just in Mexico. Observe the festivities with this sizzling selection of Mexican-inspired delights. Then cool the fire with a piece of sweet and creamy tropical pie. Olé!

PHILLY Cream Cheese Salsa Dip with tortilla chips

Ranch Taco Chicken Salad *or*
Easy Cheese Enchiladas

Sliced papaya

Pineapple Banana Coconut Cream Pie

MAXWELL HOUSE Colombian Supreme
100% Colombian Coffee

PINEAPPLE BANANA COCONUT CREAM PIE

Create a tropical paradise in your kitchen with this scrumptious dessert (photos, left and on the front cover).

Prep time: 20 minutes plus refrigerating

- 1 baked pastry shell (9 inches), cooled
- 1 large banana, sliced
- 1¾ cups cold milk
- 1 package (4-serving size) JELL-O Brand Vanilla Flavor Instant Pudding & Pie Filling
- 1½ cups BAKER'S ANGEL FLAKE Coconut
- 1 can (8 ounces) crushed pineapple, well drained
- 1 tub (8 ounces) COOL WHIP Whipped Topping, thawed
  BAKER'S ANGEL FLAKE Coconut, toasted

LINE pastry shell with banana slices.

POUR cold milk into large bowl. Add pudding mix. Beat with wire whisk 2 minutes. Stir in

1½ cups coconut. Spoon over banana slices in pastry shell. Gently stir pineapple into whipped topping. Spoon over pie. Sprinkle with toasted coconut.

REFRIGERATE 4 hours or until set. Store leftover pie in refrigerator.

Makes 8 servings.

VARIATION: Omit pastry shell. Heat oven to 325°F. Mix 1½ cups shortbread cookie crumbs (about 20 cookies), ⅔ cup BAKER'S ANGEL FLAKE Coconut and ⅓ cup butter *or* margarine, melted. Press mixture evenly into bottom and up sides of 9-inch pie plate. Bake for 10 minutes or until golden brown; cool. Prepare pie as directed.

Ranch Taco Chicken Salad (recipe, page 20)
Pineapple Banana Coconut Cream Pie

PHILLY Cream Cheese Salsa Dip

Turn the heat up or down in this recipe by choosing the salsa of your choice: mild, medium or hot.

Prep time: 5 minutes plus refrigerating

1 package (8 ounces) PHILADELPHIA BRAND Cream Cheese, softened
½ cup salsa
1 tablespoon chopped cilantro (optional)

MIX cream cheese, salsa and cilantro with electric mixer on medium speed until well blended. Refrigerate.

SERVE with tortilla chips or assorted cut-up vegetables.

Makes 2 cups.

RANCH TACO CHICKEN SALAD

Using KRAFT FREE Ranch Fat Free Dressing and KRAFT ⅓ Less Fat Natural Shredded Reduced Fat Cheddar Cheese adds flavor without extra fat. To reduce the fat even more, omit the oil and cook the chicken and chili powder in a tablespoon or two of fat-free chicken broth (photo, page 18).

Prep time: 15 minutes
Cooking time: 8 minutes

1 pound boneless skinless chicken breasts, sliced
1 tablespoon *each* oil *and* chili powder *or* Mexican seasoning
1 package (16 ounces) salad greens
1 jar (8 ounces) salsa
1 bottle (8 ounces) *or* 1 cup KRAFT Ranch Dressing *or* KRAFT FREE Ranch Fat Free Dressing
1 cup (4 ounces) KRAFT ⅓ Less Fat Natural Shredded Reduced Fat Cheddar Cheese
Broken baked tortilla chips

COOK chicken, oil and chili powder in large nonstick skillet on medium-high heat 8 minutes or until chicken is cooked through.

TOSS chicken mixture, greens, salsa, dressing and cheese in large bowl.

TOP with broken tortilla chips before serving.

Makes 6 main-dish servings.

EASY CHEESE ENCHILADAS

Some like it hot! If that's you, then add 1 or 2 chopped jalapeño or serrano peppers to the cottage cheese mixture (see note below).

Prep time: 15 minutes
Baking time: 25 minutes

- 1 container (16 ounces) BREAKSTONE'S *or* KNUDSEN Cottage Cheese
- 2 cups (8 ounces) KRAFT ⅓ Less Fat Natural Shredded Mild Reduced Fat Cheddar Cheese, divided
- ⅓ cup sliced green onions
- 2 tablespoons chopped cilantro
- 10 white corn *or* flour tortillas (6 inches), warmed
- 1 cup salsa

MIX cottage cheese, 1 cup of the cheddar cheese, onions and cilantro.

SPOON about ¼ cup of the cheese mixture down center of each tortilla; roll up. Place, seam-side down, in 12x8-inch baking dish. Top with remaining 1 cup cheddar cheese and salsa.

BAKE at 375°F for 25 minutes or until thoroughly heated.

Makes 5 servings.

Note: Chili peppers contain volatile oils that can burn your skin, lips and eyes. So, when handling hot peppers, cover one or both of your hands with plastic bags or gloves.

$\mathcal{K}$IDS—YOU'RE SPECIAL TODAY!

*Children are dear every day, but let them know it with this
kid-favorite menu—a great way to acclaim the end of the school
year or a job well done. And because it's so easy, you can use this
menu for an older child's first cooking lesson.*

Macaroni and Cheese Dinner

Carrot and cucumber sticks with
KRAFT Ranch Dip

Marshmallow Chewy Bars

Sugar-Free **KOOL-AID** Soft Drink Mix, any flavor

MARSHMALLOW CHEWY BARS

Crunchy oat cereal brings a new twist to a classic treat.

Prep time: *5 minutes plus cooling*
Microwave time: *1½ minutes OR*
Top of stove cooking time: *5 minutes*

> 2 tablespoons butter *or* margarine
> 3 cups miniature marshmallows
> 5 cups POST HONEY BUNCHES OF OATS Cereal, any
> variety

LINE 8-inch square pan with foil; lightly grease
the foil.

MICROWAVE butter in 2½-quart microwavable
bowl on HIGH 30 seconds or until butter is
melted. Add marshmallows; mix to coat.
Microwave 1 minute on HIGH or until
marshmallows are smooth when stirred, stirring
after 30 seconds.

POUR marshmallow mixture over cereal. Mix
lightly until well coated. Press firmly into
prepared pan. Cool; cut into squares. Store in
airtight container.

Makes 16.

TOP OF STOVE: Line 8-inch square pan with foil;
lightly grease foil.

Melt butter in 3-quart saucepan on low heat.
Add marshmallows; stir until marshmallows
are melted and mixture is smooth. Remove
from heat.

Pour marshmallow mixture over cereal. Mix
lightly until well coated. Press firmly into
prepared pan. Cool; cut into squares. Store in
airtight container.

*Clockwise from top left: Marshmallow Chewy Bars, Sugar-Free
KOOL-AID Soft Drink Mix, prepared **KRAFT** Ranch Sour
Cream Dip, Macaroni and Cheese Dinner (recipe, page 24)*

MACARONI AND CHEESE DINNER

VELVEETA Process Cheese Spread makes this classic dish smooth, creamy and oh-so easy—a sure-fire hit with kids of all ages (photos, right and page 22).

Prep time: 15 minutes
Baking time: 20 minutes

½ pound (8 ounces) VELVEETA Pasteurized Process Cheese Spread, cut up

¼ cup milk

1 cup (3½ ounces) elbow macaroni, cooked, drained
Dash pepper

STIR process cheese spread and milk in medium saucepan on low heat until smooth.

STIR in macaroni and pepper. Spoon into 1-quart casserole.

BAKE at 350°F for 20 minutes.

Makes 4 servings.

VARIATIONS:

For cheesier Macaroni and Cheese, increase VELVEETA Pasteurized Process Cheese Spread to ¾ pound (12 ounces). Mix ½ pound of the process cheese spread, cut up, with milk. Top casserole with remaining ¼ pound process cheese spread, sliced, before baking. Bake as directed.

For a different look, substitute bow tie pasta *or* your favorite shape for elbow macaroni.

For individual casseroles, substitute 4 (10 ounce) baking dishes for 1-quart casserole.

B E S T   O F   S P R I N G

Tomatoes

The tomato is the rare fruit that actually is used as a vegetable. It enlivens savory sauces, salads and other dishes.

When buying fresh tomatoes, look for plump, well-shaped fruit that is fairly firm-textured (but not hard), brightly colored and free of soft spots, bruises and cracks.

If fresh tomatoes are a tad hard and need ripening, place them in a brown paper bag on the kitchen counter for a few days. When they are ripe and ready-to-eat, they will yield slightly to gentle pressure.

Fresh tomatoes can be frozen, but only if you plan to use them in soups, stews and casseroles, as they soften when thawed.

Macaroni and Cheese Dinner

St. Patrick's Day Bash

*Your guests will feel as lucky as the Irish when you
serve this mid-March feast in honor of St. Patrick. Even
the not-so-Irish will enjoy traditional corned beef with
all the trimmings.*

Spinach Dip with assorted crudités

Corned beef and steamed cabbage*

Creamy Hash Potatoes

Irish soda bread*

JIGGLERS® Holiday Time Gelatin

Miniature Cheesecakes

GENERAL FOODS INTERNATIONAL COFFEES
Irish Cream Cafe Flavor

*Prepare your favorite recipe.

Spinach Dip

*This classic dip is a hit with old and young nibblers alike. Be
sure to keep a stash of fresh vegetables handy to serve with it.*

Prep time: 10 minutes plus refrigerating

- 1 package (8 ounces) PHILADELPHIA BRAND Cream Cheese, softened
- 1 cup BREAKSTONE'S *or* KNUDSEN Sour Cream
- 1 envelope GOOD SEASONS Italian Salad Dressing Mix
- 1 package (10 ounces) frozen chopped spinach, thawed, well drained
- 1 can (8 ounces) water chestnuts, drained, chopped

MIX cream cheese, sour cream and salad dressing mix with electric mixer on medium speed until well blended.

ADD remaining ingredients, mixing until well blended. Refrigerate.

SERVE with assorted cut-up vegetables.

Makes 3 cups.

Creamy Hash Potatoes (recipe, page 28)
Spinach Dip

CREAMY HASH POTATOES

Frozen hash browns make the work simple for this hearty side dish.
Serve it with roasted meats or brunch egg dishes (photo, page 26).

Prep time: 20 minutes
Baking time: 1 hour and 15 minutes

1 package (32 ounces) frozen Southern-style hash brown potatoes

1 container (16 ounces) BREAKSTONE'S *or* KNUDSEN Sour Cream

2 cups (8 ounces) KRAFT Natural *or* ⅓ Less Fat Natural Shredded Sharp Reduced Fat Cheddar Cheese

1 can (10¾ ounces) condensed cream of chicken soup

1 cup *each* chopped onion *and* corn flake crumbs

2 tablespoons butter *or* margarine, melted

MIX potatoes, sour cream, cheese, soup and onion in large bowl. Spoon into greased 3-quart casserole or 13x9-inch baking dish.

TOSS crumbs and butter; sprinkle over potato mixture.

BAKE at 350°F for 1 hour and 15 minutes.

Makes 12 servings.

JIGGLERS® HOLIDAY TIME GELATIN

The wee ones will gleefully grab for these treats made with
JELL-O Brand Gelatin. Serve JIGGLERS® for dessert or as a
between-meal snack.

Prep Time: 10 minutes plus refrigerating

2½ cups boiling water *or* boiling fruit juice (Do not add cold water or cold juice.)

2 packages (8-serving size) *or* 4 packages (4-serving size) JELL-O Brand Gelatin Dessert *or* JELL-O Brand Sugar Free Low Calorie Gelatin Dessert, any flavor

STIR boiling water into gelatin in large bowl 3 minutes or until completely dissolved. Pour into 13x9-inch pan.

REFRIGERATE at least 3 hours or until firm. (Does not stick to finger when touched.)

DIP bottom of pan in warm water about 15 seconds. Cut into decorative shapes with cookie cutters all the way through gelatin or cut into 1-inch squares. Lift from pan.

Makes about 24 pieces.

Note: Recipe can be halved. Substitute 8- or 9-inch square pan for 13x9-inch pan.

MINIATURE CHEESECAKES

You won't need special equipment to make these petite treats.
Simply use a muffin pan to downsize this popular dessert.

Prep time: 20 minutes plus refrigerating

1 package (11.2 ounces) JELL-O Brand
  No Bake Real Cheesecake

2 tablespoons sugar

⅓ cup butter *or* margarine, melted

1½ cups cold milk

  Peeled kiwi fruit slices, cut in half

MIX crumbs, sugar and butter thoroughly with fork until crumbs are well moistened. Press onto bottoms of 12 paper-lined muffin cups.

BEAT milk and filling mix with electric mixer on low speed until blended. Beat on medium speed 3 minutes. (Filling will be thick.) Spoon over crumb mixture in muffin cups.

REFRIGERATE at least 1 hour or until ready to serve. Top with kiwi. Store leftover cheesecakes in refrigerator.

Makes 12.

VARIATIONS:
For frozen cheesecakes, freeze 4 hours or overnight.

For topping variation, substitute assorted fruit, fresh mint leaves or walnuts for kiwi. Drizzle with melted BAKER'S Semi-Sweet Chocolate.

For fruit-filled cheesecakes, place small whole strawberries on crusts before adding filling. Garnish with strawberries.

MENU
Friday's Feast

*Don't wait until a Friday night
during Lent to savor this sensational
fish supper—it's a keeper any time of year!*

Lemon Dill Fish

Buttered carrots or steamed asparagus*

Tossed green salad with desired
KRAFT Pourable Dressing

Lemon Blueberry Muffins

White Chocolate Devil's Food Pie

MAXWELL HOUSE
French Vanilla Roast Flavored Ground Coffee

*Prepare your favorite recipe.

LEMON DILL FISH

*KRAFT Real Mayonnaise, lemon and dill add a tangy
essence to your favorite catch.*

Prep time: 5 minutes
Broiling time: 16 minutes

- ½ cup KRAFT Real Mayonnaise
- 1 to 2 tablespoons lemon juice
- 1 teaspoon dill weed
- ½ teaspoon grated lemon peel
- 1 pound firm-textured fish fillets
  (such as cod, catfish *or* salmon)

MIX mayonnaise, juice, dill and peel.

PLACE fish on greased rack of broiler pan
2 to 4 inches from heat. Brush with ½ of the
mayonnaise mixture.

BROIL 5 to 8 minutes. Turn; brush with
remaining mayonnaise mixture. Continue
broiling 5 to 8 minutes or until fish flakes easily
with fork.

Makes 4 servings.

Lemon Dill Fish

Lemon Blueberry Muffins

It doesn't have to be blueberry season to make these lemony fruit-filled muffins. POST BLUEBERRY MORNING Cereal with dried blueberries pinch-hits perfectly for fresh berries.

Prep time: 20 minutes
Baking time: 20 minutes

1⅓ cups flour
½ cup sugar
1 tablespoon CALUMET Baking Powder
¼ teaspoon salt
1 egg
1 cup milk
⅓ cup butter *or* margarine, melted

1½ teaspoons grated lemon peel
1½ cups POST BLUEBERRY MORNING Cereal

Mix flour, sugar, baking powder and salt in large bowl. Beat egg in small bowl; stir in milk, butter and peel. Add to flour mixture; stir just until moistened. (Batter will be lumpy.) Stir in cereal.

Spoon batter into greased or paper-lined muffin pan, filling each cup ⅔ full.

Bake in preheated 400°F oven for 20 minutes or until golden brown. Serve warm with butter, if desired.

Makes 12.

Variation: Substitute grated orange peel for lemon peel.

B E S T   O F   S P R I N G

Lemons

When buying lemons, look for those that are firm, have a nice oval shape and have smooth, evenly yellow and unblemished skin. Soft, bruised or wrinkled lemons are probably past their prime.

Good, fresh lemons will keep for 2 to 3 weeks in the crisper of your refrigerator. If you like, for future cooking needs, freeze the peel by removing it from the fruit with a vegetable peeler, shredder or grater. Spread the peel on a cookie sheet and freeze. After it's frozen, transfer the peel to freezer bags and return it to the freezer. Plan on 1 medium lemon yielding 2 teaspoons shredded peel.

WHITE CHOCOLATE DEVIL'S FOOD PIE

*When these two chocolates join forces, you
double your chocolate pleasure.*

Prep time: 20 minutes plus refrigerating

1½ cups cold skim milk, divided

1 package (4-serving size) JELL-O Brand Devil's Food
   Flavor Fat Free Instant Pudding & Pie Filling

1 tub (8 ounces) COOL WHIP LITE Whipped Topping,
   thawed

1 prepared graham cracker crumb crust
   (6 ounces *or* 9 inches)

1 package (4-serving size) JELL-O Brand White Chocolate
   Flavor Fat Free Instant Pudding & Pie Filling

POUR ¾ cup of the cold milk into medium bowl.
Add devil's food flavor pudding mix. Beat with
wire whisk 1 minute. (Mixture will be thick.)

Gently stir in ½ of the whipped topping. Spoon
into crust.

POUR remaining ¾ cup cold milk into another
medium bowl. Add white chocolate flavor
instant pudding mix. Beat with wire whisk
1 minute. (Mixture will be thick.) Gently stir in
remaining whipped topping. Spread over
pudding layer in crust.

REFRIGERATE 4 hours or until set. Sprinkle with
unsweetened cocoa, if desired. Store leftover pie
in refrigerator.

Makes 8 servings.

*M*OTHER'S DAY BRUNCH

Make Mom feel like a queen for the day with this royal springtime morning meal. Afterward, enjoy a long visit while lingering over the decadent dessert and splendid coffee you've prepared just for her.

In-season fresh fruit

Ham 'n Potatoes Au Gratin

Double Banana Bread

Bacon Morning Muffins

Luscious Lemon Poke Cake

MAXWELL HOUSE *or* **YUBAN** Coffee

HAM 'N POTATOES AU GRATIN

This dish is as welcome at brunch as it is at dinner. Choose red, russet or yellow-skinned potatoes.

Prep time: 30 minutes
Cooking time: 15 minutes

½ cup each chopped green pepper *and* chopped onion

1 tablespoon butter *or* margarine

¾ pound (12 ounces) VELVEETA Pasteurized Process Cheese Spread, cut up

⅓ cup milk

5 cups cubed cooked potatoes

1½ cups diced ham

COOK and stir green pepper and onion in butter in large skillet on medium-high heat until tender. Reduce heat to low. Add process cheese spread and milk; stir until cheese spread is melted.

STIR in remaining ingredients; heat thoroughly, stirring occasionally.

Makes 8 to 12 servings.

Ham 'n Potatoes Au Gratin
Double Banana Bread (recipe, page 36)

BACON MORNING MUFFINS

Begin your day with these delicious breakfast muffins, flavored with turkey bacon and delicately sweetened with honey.

MIX turkey bacon, flour, oats and baking powder in large bowl. Add remaining ingredients; stir just until moistened. (Batter will be lumpy.)

SPOON batter into muffin pan sprayed with no stick cooking spray or into paper-lined muffin pan, filling each cup ⅔ full.

BAKE in preheated 400°F oven for 15 minutes. Refrigerate or freeze leftover muffins. Serve with PHILADELPHIA BRAND FREE Fat Free Soft Cream Cheese with Garden Vegetables, if desired.

*Do not substitute regular pork bacon for turkey bacon in this recipe.

Makes 12.

Prep time: 10 minutes
Baking time: 15 minutes

  12 slices LOUIS RICH Turkey Bacon*, cut into ¼-inch pieces
 1¼ cups flour
   1 cup quick-cooking oats
   2 teaspoons CALUMET Baking Powder
  ½ cup skim milk
  ⅓ cup honey
  ¼ cup corn oil
   2 large egg whites

DOUBLE BANANA BREAD

The extra dose of bananas in this quick bread comes from crunchy cereal with real bananas (photo, page 34).

Prep time: 15 minutes
Baking time: 65 minutes plus cooling

 1½ cups flour
  ½ cup sugar
   2 teaspoons CALUMET Baking Powder
  ½ teaspoon baking soda
  ½ teaspoon salt
   2 eggs
 1½ cups mashed ripe bananas (2 to 3 bananas)
  ¼ cup oil
  ¼ cup water
 1½ cups POST BANANA NUT CRUNCH Cereal
   1 cup chopped walnuts (optional)

MIX flour, sugar, baking powder, baking soda and salt in large bowl. Beat eggs in medium bowl; stir in bananas, oil and water. Add to flour mixture; stir just until moistened. (Batter will be lumpy.) Stir in cereal and walnuts.

POUR into greased 9x5-inch loaf pan.

BAKE in preheated 350°F oven for 55 to 65 minutes or until toothpick inserted in center comes out clean. Cool 10 minutes; remove from pan. Cool completely on wire rack.

Makes 1 loaf.

Note: For easier slicing, wrap bread and store overnight.

LUSCIOUS LEMON POKE CAKE

This moist lemony cake is named for the way it's made. You poke the cake layers with a large fork, then pour liquid lemon-flavored gelatin over them.

Prep time: 20 minutes plus refrigerating

- 2 baked 9-inch round white cake layers, cooled
- 2 cups boiling water
- 1 package (8-serving size) *or* 2 packages (4-serving size) JELL-O Brand Lemon Flavor Gelatin Dessert
  Fluffy Lemon Pudding Frosting (recipe below)

PLACE cake layers, top sides up, in 2 clean 9-inch round cake pans. Pierce cakes with large fork at ½-inch intervals.

STIR boiling water into gelatin in medium bowl 2 minutes or until completely dissolved. Carefully pour 1 cup of the gelatin over 1 cake layer. Pour remaining gelatin over second cake layer.

REFRIGERATE 3 hours. Dip 1 cake pan in warm water 10 seconds; unmold onto serving plate. Spread top with about 1 cup of the frosting. Unmold second cake layer; carefully place on first cake layer. Frost top and sides of cake with remaining frosting.

REFRIGERATE at least 1 hour or until ready to serve. Decorate as desired. Store leftover cake in refrigerator.

Makes 12 servings.

FLUFFY LEMON PUDDING FROSTING

This delicious frosting makes enough to frost two 9-inch cake layers. Use it with the Luscious Lemon Poke Cake, above, or any other two-layer cake.

Prep time: 10 minutes

- 1 cup cold milk
- 1 package (4-serving size) JELL-O Brand Lemon Flavor Instant Pudding & Pie Filling
- ¼ cup powdered sugar
- 1 tub (8 ounces) COOL WHIP Whipped Topping, thawed

POUR cold milk into medium bowl. Add pudding mix and sugar. Beat with wire whisk 2 minutes. Gently stir in whipped topping. Immediately spread on cake.

Makes about 4 cups.

LUNCH ON THE PORCH

*Sit back and watch the birds and world go by
while dining on this selection of fresh garden delights and
easy-to-prepare foods. Make an extra batch of cookies to
share with neighbors, and your porch will be the most
popular spot on the block!*

Garden Vegetable Herb Dip with assorted
crudités and breadsticks

Vegetable Turkey Pockets

Red grapes

Crispy Oatmeal Raisin Cookies

GENERAL FOODS INTERNATIONAL COFFEES
Viennese Chocolate Cafe Flavor

GARDEN VEGETABLE HERB DIP

Create your own variations by substituting your favorite vegetables.

Prep time: 10 minutes plus refrigerating

1 container (24 ounces) BREAKSTONE'S *or*
KNUDSEN FREE Fat Free Cottage Cheese

½ cup *each* finely chopped broccoli *and* carrot

2 tablespoons *each* finely chopped green onion *and*
fresh parsley

1 envelope GOOD SEASONS Italian Salad Dressing Mix

PLACE cottage cheese in blender or food processor container; cover. Blend on low speed until pureed.

STIR in remaining ingredients. Refrigerate.

SERVE with assorted cut-up vegetables or breadsticks.

Makes 4 cups.

Vegetable Turkey Pockets (recipe, page 40)
Garden Vegetable Herb Dip

VEGETABLE TURKEY POCKETS

Carry these sandwiches to work and treat a few coworkers to lunch! Pack the turkey mixture in an airtight container and chill until lunchtime. Then spoon it into the pita breads just before eating (photo, page 38).

Prep time: 20 minutes plus refrigerating

¼ cup SEVEN SEAS ⅓ Less Fat Ranch Dressing

¼ cup KRAFT LIGHT Mayonnaise Dressing

8 slices LOUIS RICH Oven Roasted Turkey Breast, cut into strips

½ cup chopped cucumber

½ cup shredded carrot

1 small tomato, chopped

1 teaspoon dried basil leaves, crushed

2 pita breads, cut in half

Lettuce leaves

MIX dressings, turkey, cucumber, carrot, tomato and basil. Refrigerate.

FILL pita bread halves with lettuce and turkey mixture.

Makes 4 sandwiches.

BEST OF SPRING

Carrots

Although there are hundreds of varieties of carrots, they are categorized for the kitchen by their shape and size rather than their variety. In addition to the familiar long and slender orange carrots, baby carrots are also available. These may be round, may look like miniature versions of regular-size carrots and may either be orange or creamy white in color.

No matter what the shape of your favorite kind of carrot, always select those that are straight, rigid, bright orange or white and have no cracks or dry, white spots. If carrots have their tops still attached, the tops should be green and fresh.

Cut off carrot tops, if they're attached, for storage. All carrots can be refrigerated in plastic bags for up to 2 weeks. For longer storage, first blanch trimmed, peeled, whole or cut-up carrots. Then pack them in freezer containers and freeze for up to a year.

For cooking purposes, figure 1 pound equals 6 to 8 medium-size carrots, and 2 medium-size carrots equal 1 cup sliced.

CRISPY OATMEAL RAISIN COOKIES

*POST GRAPE-NUTS Cereal gives a winning crunchiness to these
classic oatmeal-raisin cookies.*

Prep time: 15 minutes
Baking time per cookie sheet: 8 minutes plus cooling

1½ cups flour
1 teaspoon baking soda
1½ cups (3 sticks) butter *or* margarine, softened
⅔ cup *each* firmly packed brown sugar *and* granulated
    sugar
1 egg
1 teaspoon vanilla
2 cups POST GRAPE-NUTS Cereal
2 cups quick-cooking oats
1 cup raisins

MIX flour and baking soda in small bowl. Beat butter in large bowl with electric mixer on medium speed to soften. Gradually add sugars, beating until light and fluffy. Beat in egg and vanilla. Gradually add flour mixture, beating well after each addition. Stir in cereal, oats and raisins.

DROP by rounded tablespoonfuls onto ungreased cookie sheets.

BAKE in preheated 375°F oven for 8 minutes or until lightly browned. Cool 1 minute; remove from cookie sheets. Cool cookies completely on wire racks.

Makes 5 dozen.

DINNER ALFRESCO

Alfresco *means "occuring in the open air"—
and that's where you'll want to be while enjoying this
remarkable fare. Your backyard deck or patio provides the
ideal stage and a warm spring night is the perfect
backdrop for this Italy-inspired evening.*

Plum Tomato and Pesto Bread

Shrimp Tortellini Primavera

Sliced tomatoes with fresh basil

PHILLY 3-STEP™ Luscious Lemon
Cheesecake

Cafe Diablo (recipe, page 7)

PLUM TOMATO AND PESTO BREAD

*Plum tomatoes, also called roma tomatoes, are flavorful egg-shaped
fruit that come in shades of red and yellow. They make a
colorful addition to this side dish or appetizer.*

Prep time: 15 minutes
Baking time: 20 minutes

- 1 loaf (about 16 ounces) Italian bread, cut in half lengthwise
- 1 package (7 ounces) DI GIORNO Pesto Sauce
- 6 plum tomatoes, sliced
- ½ cup sliced pitted ripe olives
- 2 cups (8 ounces) KRAFT Natural Shredded Low-Moisture Part-Skim Mozzarella Cheese
- ½ cup (2 ounces) DI GIORNO 100% Shredded Parmesan Cheese

PLACE bread, cut-side up, on cookie sheet. Bake in preheated 400°F oven for 8 to 10 minutes or until golden brown.

SPREAD each bread half with pesto sauce; top with tomato slices. Sprinkle with olives and cheeses.

BAKE at 400°F for 8 to 10 minutes or until cheeses are melted. Cut into slices.

Makes about 24 servings.

Shrimp Tortellini Primavera (recipe, page 44)
Plum Tomato and Pesto Bread

SHRIMP TORTELLINI PRIMAVERA

Primavera is Italian for "spring style." With its bright-hued vegetables and the freshness of DI GIORNO Pasta and Sauce, this quick dish lives up to its name (photo, page 42).

Prep time: 5 minutes
Cooking time: 5 minutes

- 1 package (9 ounces) DI GIORNO Cheese Tortellini
- 2 cups frozen assorted vegetables
- 1 package (10 ounces) frozen cooked shrimp, thawed
- 1 package (7 ounces) DI GIORNO Olive Oil and Garlic Sauce

ADD tortellini to 4 quarts boiling water. Boil gently, 2 minutes, stirring frequently.

STIR in vegetables. Continue cooking 3 minutes; drain.

TOSS immediately with remaining ingredients.

Makes 4 servings.

PHILLY 3-STEP™ LUSCIOUS LEMON CHEESECAKE

Here's a deceptively simple dessert. All you have to do is mix, pour and bake—then sit back and enjoy the praise!

Prep time: 10 minutes
Baking time: 40 minutes

- 2 packages (8 ounces each) PHILADELPHIA BRAND Cream Cheese, softened
- ½ cup sugar
- 1 tablespoon fresh lemon juice
- ½ teaspoon grated lemon peel
- ½ teaspoon vanilla
- 2 eggs
- 1 ready-to-use graham cracker crumb crust (6 ounces or 9 inches)

1. MIX cream cheese, sugar, juice, peel and vanilla with electric mixer on medium speed until well blended. Add eggs; mix until blended.

2. POUR into crust.

3. BAKE at 350°F for 40 minutes or until center is almost set. Cool. Refrigerate 3 hours or overnight. Garnish with fresh raspberries, lemon slices and mint, if desired.

Makes 8 servings.

VARIATIONS:
For a fruit-topped cheesecake, omit juice and peel. Top refrigerated cheesecake with 2 cups sliced assorted fresh fruit.

For a lower fat version, substitute PHILADELPHIA BRAND Neufchatel Cheese, ⅓ Less Fat than Cream Cheese, for regular cream cheese.

PHILLY 3-STEP™ Luscious Lemon Cheesecake
Cafe Diablo (recipe, page 7)

SPRINGTIME SALAD BUFFET

Planning a luncheon, wedding shower or graduation open house? This artful array of garden salads is sure to please any crowd for almost any springtime occasion.

Tomato Basil 'n Cheddar Snacks

Chicken Caesar Salad

Ham and Pineapple Ranch Salad

Italian Tuna Salad on Greens

Heartland Layered Salad

Assorted rolls

Creamy Pudding Sauce with fresh fruit

Iced Russian Tea (recipe, page 61)

HEARTLAND LAYERED SALAD

The freshness of layered garden vegetables is sealed in with KRAFT Ranch Dressing, keeping this salad bright and crisp until it's ready to serve.

Prep time: 20 minutes plus refrigerating

4 cups chopped lettuce

1 cup chopped tomato

½ cup chopped green onions

1 can (11 ounces) whole kernel corn, drained

1 bottle (8 ounces) *or* 1 cup KRAFT Ranch Dressing

1 cup (4 ounces) KRAFT Natural Shredded Cheddar Cheese

8 slices OSCAR MAYER Bacon, crisply cooked, crumbled

LAYER lettuce, tomato, onions and corn in 1½-quart glass bowl.

SPREAD dressing over corn, sealing to edges of bowl. Sprinkle with cheese; cover. Refrigerate several hours or overnight.

SPRINKLE with bacon just before serving.

Makes 6 side-dish servings.

From top left: Heartland Layered Salad, Iced Russian Tea (recipe, page 61), Chicken Caesar Salad (recipe, page 48), Tomato Basil 'n Cheddar Snacks (recipe, page 49)

Chicken Caesar Salad

*Making this ever-popular restaurant salad at home is simple
with KRAFT Caesar Ranch Dressing and KRAFT 100% Shredded
Parmesan Cheese (photo, page 46).*

Prep time: 20 minutes
Cooking time: 10 minutes

- 4 boneless skinless chicken breast halves
  (about 1¼ pounds), cut into strips
- 2 cloves garlic, minced
- 1 tablespoon oil
- 1 bottle (8 ounces) *or* 1 cup KRAFT Caesar Ranch
  Dressing or KRAFT FREE Ranch Fat Free Dressing
- 1¼ cups (5 ounces) KRAFT 100% Shredded
  Parmesan Cheese
- 6 cups torn romaine lettuce
- 1 small red onion, sliced, separated into rings
- 1½ cups seasoned croutons

Fresh lemon wedges
Coarse grind black pepper

Cook chicken and garlic in oil in large skillet on
medium heat until chicken is cooked through.

Mix dressing and Parmesan cheese.

Toss lettuce, onion, croutons and chicken in
large salad bowl. Pour dressing mixture over
salad; toss to coat. Spoon onto serving platter.
Serve with fresh lemon and pepper.

Makes 6 main-dish servings.

Ham and Pineapple Ranch Salad

*With asparagus for character, pineapple for sweetness and chow
mein noodles for fun, your guests are sure to come back for seconds!*

Prep time: 15 minutes

- ½ pound ham, julienne-cut
- 1 can (8 ounces) pineapple chunks, drained
- 1 cup asparagus tips, fresh *or* frozen, blanched
- 1 package (10 ounces) salad greens
  KRAFT FREE Ranch Fat Free Dressing
- ½ cup chow mein noodles

Arrange ham, pineapple and asparagus over
greens.

Serve with dressing. Sprinkle with chow mein
noodles.

Makes 6 main-dish servings.

Italian Tuna Salad on Greens

If you can't find fresh green beans, use one 9- or 10-ounce package of frozen green beans. Cook according to package directions, then cool before using.

Prep time: 10 minutes

- 1 can (14 ounces) artichoke hearts, drained, quartered
- 1 can (9¼ ounces) tuna in water, drained, flaked
- ½ pound green beans, cooked, drained
- 1 cup sliced plum tomatoes
- 1 package (10 ounces) salad greens
- 1 bottle (8 ounces) *or* 1 cup KRAFT Italian Dressing *or* KRAFT FREE Italian Fat Free Dressing

ARRANGE artichokes, tuna, beans and tomatoes on greens.

SERVE with dressing.

Makes 6 main-dish servings.

Tomato Basil 'n Cheddar Snacks

Keep plenty of these ingredients on hand to replenish this speedy appetizer in a flash (photo, page 46).

Prep time: 10 minutes

- 28 crackers
- 1 package (10 ounces) CRACKER BARREL Extra Sharp Natural Cheddar Cheese, thinly sliced
- 28 fresh basil leaves *or* ½ teaspoon dried basil leaves
- 28 slices cherry tomato (about 7 cherry tomatoes)

TOP each cracker with 1 cheese slice, basil and 1 tomato slice.

Makes 28.

Creamy Pudding Sauce

Presto! In minutes, this creamy sauce can be your answer to that all-time question, "What's for dessert?" It's superb spooned over fresh fruit or pound cake.

Prep time: 5 minutes plus standing

- 3½ cups cold skim milk
- 1 package (4-serving size) JELL-O Brand Devil's Food *or* White Chocolate Flavor Fat Free Instant Pudding & Pie Filling

POUR cold milk into medium bowl. Add pudding mix. Beat with wire whisk 1 minute. Let stand 10 minutes or until slightly thickened.

SERVE with assorted fresh fruit. Store leftover sauce in refrigerator.

Makes 3½ cups.

Note: Thin with small amount of additional milk before serving, if desired.

Mardi Gras Dinner

Feast now, fast later—that's the lighthearted philosophy behind this celebrated Tuesday before Lent. However, this festive menu is fun and filling anytime of the year.

One-Dish Chicken & **STOVE TOP** Bake

Candied yams*

Spinach Bacon Salad

Candy Bar Pie

MAXWELL HOUSE 1892 Slow Roasted Coffee

*Prepare your favorite recipe.

One-Dish Chicken & STOVE TOP Bake

After you've tried this easy dish for your Mardi Gras Dinner, you'll find it's a sure bet as a satisfying family-pleaser year-round.

Prep time: 10 minutes
Baking time: 35 minutes

- 1 package (6 ounces) STOVE TOP Stuffing Mix for Chicken
- 4 boneless skinless chicken breast halves (about 1¼ pounds)
- 1 can (10¾ ounces) condensed cream of mushroom soup
- ⅓ cup BREAKSTONE'S *or* KNUDSEN Sour Cream *or* milk

PREPARE stuffing mix as directed on package; set aside.

PLACE chicken in 2-quart casserole or 12x8-inch baking dish. Mix soup and sour cream; pour over chicken. Spoon stuffing evenly over top.

BAKE at 375°F for 35 minutes or until chicken is cooked through.

Makes 4 servings.

*One-Dish Chicken & **STOVE TOP** Bake*
Spinach Bacon Salad (recipe, page 52)

SPINACH BACON SALAD

Turkey bacon adds a lower-fat twist and loads of flavor to this springtime favorite.
For more crunch, serve with garlic-flavored croutons (photo, page 50).

Prep time: 10 minutes
Cooking time: 13 minutes

8 slices LOUIS RICH Turkey Bacon, cut into 1-inch pieces
½ large red onion, coarsely chopped
¼ cup water
3 tablespoons sugar
2 tablespoons vinegar
⅛ teaspoon pepper
6 cups torn spinach *or* small spinach leaves

HEAT turkey bacon and onion in large nonstick skillet on medium heat 10 minutes or until turkey bacon begins to brown, stirring occasionally.

MIX water, sugar, vinegar and pepper. Stir into turkey bacon mixture. Reduce heat to low; simmer 3 minutes.

PLACE spinach in large serving bowl. Pour turkey bacon mixture over spinach; toss to coat.

Makes 4 side-dish servings.

CANDY BAR PIE

Enjoy this candy-studded pie at your Mardi Gras Dinner
or at any party celebration.

Prep time: 20 minutes plus refrigerating

4 ounces PHILADELPHIA BRAND Cream Cheese, softened
1 tablespoon milk *or* half-and-half
1 tub (12 ounces) COOL WHIP Whipped Topping, thawed
2 packages (2.07 ounces each) chocolate-covered caramel peanut nougat bars, chopped
1½ cups cold milk *or* half-and-half
2 packages (4-serving size each) JELL-O Brand Chocolate Flavor Instant Pudding & Pie Filling
1 prepared chocolate flavor crumb crust (6 ounces)

MIX cream cheese and 1 tablespoon milk in large bowl with wire whisk until smooth. Gently stir in 1½ cups of the whipped topping and chopped candy bars.

POUR 1½ cups cold milk into another large bowl. Add pudding mixes. Beat with wire whisk 1 minute. (Mixture will be thick.) Gently stir in 2 cups of the whipped topping. Spread ½ of the pudding mixture on bottom of crust. Spread cream cheese mixture over pudding mixture in crust. Spread remaining pudding mixture over cream cheese layer.

REFRIGERATE 4 hours or until set. Pipe remaining whipped topping around edge of pie. Sprinkle with shaved chocolate and garnish with piped white and dark chocolate swirls, if desired. Store leftover pie in refrigerator.

Makes 8 servings.

Candy Bar Pie

FAMILY VIDEO NIGHT SUPPER

Treat movie-watchers to this menu of all-time classics. But watch out—these family-pleasing munchies might rival the movie as the evening's featured attraction.

Tuna Sandwich Melts *or*
Cottage Cheese and Vegetable Topped Potato

Apple slices and green grapes

Peanut Butter Drop Cookies *or*
Coconut Macaroons

Sugar-Free **KOOL-AID** Soft Drink Mix, any flavor

TUNA SANDWICH MELTS

*Crisp Kaiser rolls create a twist on the traditional tuna melt—
and turn these sandwiches into perfect fare for munching
in front of the television set.*

Prep time: 15 minutes
Baking time: 25 minutes OR
Microwave time: 2 minutes

- 1 can (6⅛ ounces) tuna in water, drained, flaked
- ½ cup MIRACLE WHIP Salad Dressing
- ¼ pound (4 ounces) VELVEETA Pasteurized Process Cheese Spread, cut up
- ½ cup sliced celery
- ¼ cup chopped onion
- 4 Kaiser rolls, split

MIX all ingredients except rolls.

FILL each roll with ⅓ cup tuna mixture; wrap in foil.

BAKE at 375°F for 20 to 25 minutes or until thoroughly heated.

Makes 4 sandwiches.

MICROWAVE: Prepare sandwiches as directed, except for wrapping in foil. Place 2 sandwiches on paper towel. Microwave on HIGH 1 minute or until thoroughly heated. Repeat with remaining sandwiches.

*From top right: Sugar-Free **KOOL-AID** Soft Drink Mix,
Peanut Butter Drop Cookies (recipe, page 56), Tuna
Sandwich Melts*

COTTAGE CHEESE AND VEGETABLE TOPPED POTATO

For baking, russet or Idaho potatoes will give you the best results. Bake them at 425°F for 40 to 60 minutes. Or, microwave them on HIGH. Allow 5 to 7 minutes for one potato or 13 to 16 minutes for four potatoes, rearranging and turning the potatoes over once.

Prep time: 10 minutes

- 1 hot baked potato, split
- ½ cup cooked sliced carrots, red pepper strips *and* halved sliced zucchini
- ½ cup BREAKSTONE'S *or* KNUDSEN Cottage Cheese

TOP potato with vegetables and cottage cheese. Garnish with fresh chives.

Makes 1 serving.

PEANUT BUTTER DROP COOKIES

These gems offer a kid-pleasing crunch (photo, page 54).

Prep time: 15 minutes
Baking time per cookie sheet: 12 minutes plus cooling

- 1¼ cups flour
- 1 teaspoon baking soda
- ¼ teaspoon salt
- ½ cup (1 stick) butter *or* margarine, softened
- 1 cup sugar
- 1 egg
- 1 teaspoon vanilla
- ½ cup peanut butter
- 2 tablespoons milk
- 1½ cups POST HONEY BUNCHES OF OATS Cereal, any variety

MIX flour, baking soda and salt in small bowl. Beat butter in large bowl with electric mixer on medium speed to soften. Gradually add sugar, beating until light and fluffy. Beat in egg, vanilla and peanut butter. Gradually add flour mixture alternately with milk, beating well after each addition. Stir in cereal.

DROP by heaping teaspoonfuls onto ungreased cookie sheets.

BAKE in preheated 350°F oven for 10 to 12 minutes or until edges are golden brown. Cool slightly. Remove from cookie sheets. Cool on wire racks.

Makes 4 dozen.

COCONUT MACAROONS

Dip these coconut puffs into chocolate for an exceptional treat.

Prep time: 10 minutes
Baking time per cookie sheet: 20 minutes plus cooling

2⅔ cups (7 ounces) BAKER'S ANGEL FLAKE Coconut

⅔ cup sugar

6 tablespoons flour

¼ teaspoon salt

4 egg whites

1 teaspoon almond extract

Whole candied cherries *or* whole natural almonds
(optional)

MIX coconut, sugar, flour and salt in large bowl. Stir in egg whites and almond extract until well blended.

DROP by teaspoonfuls onto greased and floured cookie sheets. Press 1 candied cherry or almond into center of each cookie, if desired.

BAKE in preheated 325°F oven for 20 minutes or until edges of cookies are golden brown. Immediately remove from cookie sheets. Cool on wire racks.

Makes about 3 dozen.

CHOCOLATE-DIPPED MACAROONS: Prepare Coconut Macaroons as directed. Cool. Melt 1 package (8 squares) BAKER'S Semi-Sweet Chocolate as directed on package. Dip cookies halfway into chocolate; let excess chocolate drip off. Let stand at room temperature or refrigerate on wax paper-lined tray 30 minutes or until chocolate is firm.

BEST OF SPRING

Potatoes

The potato is one of nature's most versatile foods. Depending on the variety, a potato can have skin that is brown, yellow, white, red or purple, and a crisp meat that usually is either white or yellow, but always creamy and satisfying when cooked.

Store potatoes in a cool, dark place that's humid—but not wet—and well-ventilated. This will reward you with potatoes that have good flavor and texture for several weeks. Long periods of exposure to light will cause the potato skin to turn green and develop a bitter flavor. Slightly green potatoes are safe to eat, but it's best to remove the discolored areas. Severely greened potatoes can be toxic, but the bitterness will keep you from eating enough to cause harm. Don't refrigerate potatoes. They'll become unappealingly sweet and may darken when cooked.

Derby Day Dinner Buffet

Even if your horses don't finish in the money,
everyone's a winner with this first-rate buffet.

Sour Cream Pesto Dip with Tortelloni

Grilled beef tenderloin*

American Potato Salad

Mixed baby salad greens with desired **KRAFT**
pourable dressing

Cheesy Garlic Bread

PHILLY Cream Cheese Classic Cheesecake
with fresh berries

Iced Russian Tea *or*
MAXWELL HOUSE Coffee Cappuccino

*Prepare your favorite recipe.

Sour Cream Pesto Dip with Tortelloni

Everyone will think you spent hours in the kitchen on this hearty
Italian appetizer, but it takes only minutes.

Prep time: 10 minutes
Cooking time: 6 minutes

- 1 package (9 ounces) DI GIORNO Mushroom Tortelloni
- 1 package (9 ounces) DI GIORNO Hot Red Pepper Cheese Tortelloni
- 1 package (7 ounces) DI GIORNO Pesto Sauce
- 1 cup BREAKSTONE'S *or* KNUDSEN Sour Cream
  Green *and* red pepper strips
  Pitted ripe olives

ADD both packages of tortelloni to 4 quarts boiling water. Boil gently, uncovered, 6 minutes, stirring frequently. Drain; rinse with cold water.

MIX pesto sauce and sour cream in small bowl.

PLACE bowl in center of a serving platter. Arrange tortelloni, peppers and olives around bowl.

Makes 24 servings.

American Potato Salad (recipe, page 60)
Sour Cream Pesto Dip with Tortelloni

American Potato Salad

*For best results, cook the potatoes whole and cube them
when they are cool enough to handle (photo, page 58).*

Prep time: 30 minutes plus refrigerating

- ¾ cup MIRACLE WHIP *or*
  MIRACLE WHIP LIGHT Dressing
- 1 teaspoon KRAFT Pure Prepared Mustard
- ½ teaspoon celery seed
- ½ teaspoon salt
- ⅛ teaspoon pepper
- 4 cups cubed cooked potatoes
- 2 hard-cooked eggs, chopped
- ½ cup *each* chopped onion, chopped sweet pickles *and*
  sliced celery

Mix dressing, mustard and seasonings in
large bowl.

Add remaining ingredients; mix lightly.
Refrigerate.

Makes 6 side-dish servings.

Variations:

For a ham and potato salad, omit pickles and
celery. Add 1½ cups chopped ham and ½ cup
chopped green pepper.

For a dill-flavored salad, omit celery seed,
pickles and celery. Add 1 cup chopped
cucumber and ½ teaspoon dill weed.

Cheesy Garlic Bread

*If you have avid garlic-lovers at your house, increase the amount of
garlic in this cheese spread to three or four cloves.*

Prep time: 10 minutes
Broiling time: 3 minutes

- 2 cups (8 ounces) KRAFT Natural Shredded Low-Moisture
  Part-Skim Mozzarella Cheese
- ¾ cup (1½ sticks) butter *or* margarine, softened
- 1 clove garlic, minced
- 1 loaf Italian bread, cut in half lengthwise

Mix cheese, butter and garlic until well blended.

Spread on cut surfaces of bread.

Broil 2 to 3 minutes or until cheese mixture is
bubbly. Sprinkle with fresh oregano leaves, if
desired. Cut into slices.

Makes 20 servings.

RUSSIAN TEA MIX

Fill your teacup with orange and spice and everything nice!
Serve it hot or cold (photos, below and pages 10 and 46).

Prep time: 10 minutes

1⅓ cups TANG Brand Orange Flavor Drink Mix

½ cup sugar

⅓ cup instant tea

1 teaspoon ground cinnamon

½ teaspoon ground cloves

MIX all ingredients. Store in tightly covered jar.

Makes 2 cups mix.

For 1 serving, place 1 tablespoon mix into cup. Add ¾ cup boiling water. Stir until mix is dissolved.

For 4 servings (1 quart), place ⅓ cup mix into heatproof pitcher or bowl. Add 4 cups (1 quart) boiling water. Stir until mix is dissolved. Serve with lemon wedges, if desired.

VARIATIONS:

For 1 serving of Iced Russian Tea, dissolve 2 tablespoons tea mix in ¾ cup boiling water. Pour over ice cubes in tall glass.

For a reduced-sugar version, reduce sugar to ¼ cup. Substitute 1 cup TANG Brand Orange Flavor Sugar Free Drink Mix for regular drink mix.

PHILLY Cream Cheese Classic Cheesecake

This foolproof dessert won't disappoint you or your guests. To add a glamorous garnish, see the tips on candied flowers, pages 86–87 (photos, right and on the cover).

Prep time: 20 minutes
Baking time: 55 minutes

1½ cups graham cracker crumbs

3 tablespoons sugar

⅓ cup butter *or* margarine, melted

4 packages (8 ounces each) PHILADELPHIA BRAND Cream Cheese, softened

1 cup sugar

1 teaspoon vanilla

4 eggs

MIX crumbs, 3 tablespoons sugar and butter. Press onto bottom of 9-inch springform pan.

MIX cream cheese, 1 cup sugar and vanilla with electric mixer on medium speed until well blended. Add eggs; mix until blended. Pour over crust in pan.

BAKE in preheated 350°F oven for 55 minutes or until center is almost set. Loosen cake from rim of pan; cool before removing rim of pan. Refrigerate. Top with fresh fruit, if desired.

Makes 12 servings.

BEST OF SPRING

Kiwi Fruit

Once considered quite exotic, kiwi fruit is now commonly available—but is still uncommonly delicious. The brown, fuzzy-skinned, egg-shaped exterior of the fruit yields to a lime-green interior that is delicately flecked with tiny black seeds.

The flavor of the kiwi is slightly sweet and seemingly a mingling of strawberries, melon and another fuzzy-skinned fruit—peaches.

When kiwi fruit is ready to be eaten, it should yield slightly to gentle pressure and should have an exterior free of bruises or extremely soft spots. If it does not yield to gentle pressure, ripen the fruit on the kitchen counter at room temperature. Once ripe, kiwi fruit may be kept in the refrigerator for up to a week.

Although its fuzz is more prominent than that of a peach, you can eat a kiwi without peeling it—just rub the brown skin gently with a clean cloth to get rid of the bothersome excess fuzz.

PHILLY Cream Cheese Classic Cheesecake

WHEN THE MARCH WIND BLOWS

When it's cold outside, stay warm inside by feasting on this menu of cozy comfort foods. Top off the evening with steaming cups of hot flavored coffee.

Easy Chicken Pot Pie

Strawberry and Banana Salad

All-Time Favorite Puff Pudding

GENERAL FOODS INTERNATIONAL COFFEES
Cafe Vienna Flavor

EASY CHICKEN POT PIE

This easy-on-the-cook casserole is an excellent home-style warmer for a blustery spring day. Indulge yourself!

Prep time: 15 minutes
Baking time: 45 minutes

- 1 package (6 ounces) STOVE TOP Stuffing Mix for Chicken
- 1½ cups hot water
- ¼ cup (½ stick) butter *or* margarine, cut into pieces
- 2 cups cubed cooked chicken
- 1 jar (12 ounces) chicken gravy
- 1 package (10 ounces) frozen mixed vegetables, thawed, drained
- ¼ teaspoon dried thyme leaves

MIX contents of vegetable/seasoning packet, hot water and butter in large bowl until butter is melted. Stir in stuffing crumbs just to moisten. Let stand 5 minutes.

MIX chicken, gravy, vegetables and thyme in 2-quart casserole or 12x8-inch baking dish. Spoon stuffing evenly over chicken mixture.

BAKE at 350°F for 45 minutes or until thoroughly heated.

Makes 6 servings.

Easy Chicken Pot Pie
Strawberry and Banana Salad (recipe, page 66)

STRAWBERRY AND BANANA SALAD

This refreshing and pretty JELL-O salad will bring to mind the brighter days of spring that are just around the corner (photo, page 64).

Prep time: 10 minutes plus refrigerating

1½ cups boiling water

1 package (8-serving size) *or* 2 packages (4-serving size) JELL-O Brand Strawberry Flavor Gelatin Dessert

1 cup cold water

Ice cubes

2 medium bananas, sliced

STIR boiling water into gelatin in large bowl 2 minutes or until completely dissolved. Mix cold water and ice cubes to make 2½ cups. Add to gelatin, stirring until slightly thickened. Remove any remaining ice. Stir in bananas. Pour into 6-cup ring mold or serving bowl.

REFRIGERATE 2 hours or until firm. Unmold. Garnish as desired. Store leftover salad in refrigerator.

Makes 8 to 10 side-dish servings.

Note: To unmold the salad, dip mold in warm water for about 15 seconds. Gently pull gelatin from around edges with moist fingers. Place moistened serving plate on top of mold. Invert mold and plate; holding mold and plate together, shake slightly to loosen. Gently remove mold and center gelatin on plate.

BEST OF SPRING

Strawberries

The much-favored strawberry is a sweet, soft, heart-shaped, vibrantly red berry that wears a bright green cap when it's fresh. Make sure you pick the plumpest, reddest, most fully ripened strawberries you can lay your hands on, as they don't ripen after they are picked. And remember, the biggest berries are not necessarily the sweetest and juiciest. The smaller ones—as long as they're not bruised, wet or mushy—can be just as sweet as the bigger ones.

Once you have them home from the supermarket or berry patch, simply store them in a single layer, loosely covered, in the refrigerator until you're ready to use them. Because strawberries are highly perishable, they need to be used within 1 to 2 days. Just before you're ready to eat them, wash and hull the berries.

If it will be longer than 2 days, you can freeze strawberries by arranging washed berries on a cookie sheet. Then place the cookie sheet in the freezer until the strawberries are solid. When they're solid, transfer the berries to a plastic freezer container or bag, leaving ½-inch headspace. Return them to the freezer.

ALL-TIME FAVORITE PUFF PUDDING

*This dessert is called puff pudding because after it bakes
you'll find a puffy, cake-like texture on top and a creamy
custard on the bottom.*

Prep time: 15 minutes
Baking time: 1 hour and 15 minutes

  1 cup sugar
  ½ cup (1 stick) butter *or* margarine, softened
  4 egg yolks
  2 cups milk
  ½ cup POST GRAPE-NUTS Cereal
  ¼ cup flour
  ¼ cup lemon juice
  2 teaspoons grated lemon peel
  4 egg whites, stiffly beaten

BEAT sugar and butter in large bowl with electric mixer on medium speed until light and fluffy. Beat in egg yolks.

STIR in milk, cereal, flour, juice and peel. (Mixture will look curdled.) Gently stir in stiffly beaten egg whites. Pour into greased 2-quart baking dish. Place dish in large baking pan. Fill pan with hot water to depth of 1 inch.

BAKE in preheated 350°F oven for 1 hour and 15 minutes or until top is golden brown and begins to pull away from sides of dish. (Pudding will have cake-like layer on top with custard below.) Serve warm or cold with cream or whipped topping, if desired.

Makes 10 servings.

VARIATION: For individual puddings, pour mixture into 10 custard cups. Bake 40 minutes.

AFTER-THE-GAME BUFFET

Big and little leaguers alike will come running home for this all-star lineup. And thanks to the make-ahead dessert and salad, this post-game spread goes together in a flash.

California Club Sandwiches

Tangy Broccoli Salad

ONE BOWL® Cream Cheese Brownies

Orange Banana Shake

MAXWELL HOUSE Mocha Cappuccino

CALIFORNIA CLUB SANDWICHES

Decked out with turkey, avocado, alfalfa sprouts, tomatoes and a smooth mustard-honey mayonnaise, this special sandwich is West-Coast wonderful.

Prep time: 10 minutes

- ½ cup KRAFT Real Mayonnaise
- 2 teaspoons Dijon mustard
- 2 teaspoons honey
- 12 whole wheat bread slices, toasted
- 2 packages (5.5 ounces each) LOUIS RICH CARVING BOARD Oven Roasted Turkey Breast
- 1 avocado, thinly sliced
- 1 cup alfalfa sprouts
- 1 large tomato, thinly sliced

MIX mayonnaise, mustard and honey in small bowl. Spread 1 side of each toast slice with mayonnaise mixture.

LAYER 4 toast slices each with turkey, avocado and second toast slice. Top each with sprouts, tomato and third toast slice.

Makes 4 sandwiches.

Tangy Broccoli Salad (recipe, page 70)
California Club Sandwiches

Tangy Broccoli Salad

*Sweet raisins complement the tang of the dressing in this easy
vegetable salad (photo, page 68).*

Prep time: 20 minutes plus refrigerating

- 1 cup MIRACLE WHIP *or* MIRACLE WHIP LIGHT Dressing
- 2 tablespoons sugar
- 2 tablespoons vinegar
- 1 medium bunch broccoli, cut into flowerets (about 6 cups)
- 4 cups loosely packed fresh spinach leaves
- 12 slices OSCAR MAYER Bacon, crisply cooked, crumbled
- ½ cup red onion rings
- ¼ cup raisins

Mix dressing, sugar and vinegar in large bowl.

Add remaining ingredients; mix lightly. Refrigerate.

Makes 8 side-dish servings.

Orange Banana Shake

*Get an energy boost after a game—or anytime—with this
refreshing orange-flavored drink.*

Prep time: 5 minutes

- ½ cup milk
- ⅓ cup water
- ¼ cup TANG Brand Orange Flavor Drink Mix
- 1 fully ripe medium banana, cut up
- 3 ice cubes *or* ½ cup crushed ice

Place milk, water and drink mix in blender container; cover. Blend on high speed 30 seconds.

Add banana and ice cubes; cover. Blend on high speed 30 seconds or until smooth. Serve immediately.

Makes 1⅔ cups or 2 servings.

ONE BOWL® CREAM CHEESE BROWNIES

*The key to making these rich, fudgy brownies is to avoid
overbaking them.*

Prep time: 20 minutes
Microwave time: 2 minutes
Baking time: 40 minutes plus cooling

    4 squares BAKER'S Unsweetened Chocolate

  ¾ cup (1½ sticks) butter *or* margarine

    2 cups sugar

    4 eggs

    I teaspoon vanilla

    I cup flour

    I cup coarsely chopped nuts (optional)

    I package (8 ounces) PHILADELPHIA BRAND Cream
       Cheese, softened

  ⅓ cup sugar

    I egg

    2 tablespoons flour

MICROWAVE chocolate and butter in large microwavable bowl on HIGH 2 minutes or until butter is melted. Stir until chocolate is completely melted.

STIR 2 cups sugar into chocolate until well blended. Mix in 4 eggs and vanilla. Stir in 1 cup flour and nuts until well blended. Spread in greased 13x9-inch baking pan.

BEAT cream cheese, ⅓ cup sugar, 1 egg and 2 tablespoons flour in same bowl until well blended. Spoon mixture over brownie batter. Cut through batter with knife several times to create marble effect.

BAKE in preheated 350°F oven (325°F for glass baking dish) for 40 minutes or until toothpick inserted in center comes out with fudgy crumbs. DO NOT OVERBAKE. Cool in pan. Cut into squares.

Makes 2 dozen.

ℋOUSEWARMING WELCOME

*Nothing says "welcome" to a new neighbor more than a
gift from your kitchen. Choose from these three home-style
hearth-warmers to ease the moving-day dinner crunch.*

Turkey and Green Bean Casserole *or*

Easy Classic Lasagna *or*

Chicken Sour Cream Enchiladas

TURKEY AND GREEN BEAN CASSEROLE

*Offer this welcoming Thanksgiving-like dish to new
neighbors, and they'll be thankful for your thoughtfulness.*

Prep time: 10 minutes
Baking time: 30 minutes

1	package (6 ounces) STOVE TOP Savory Herb Stuffing Mix or Stuffing Mix for Turkey
1½	cups hot water
¼	cup (½ stick) butter or margarine, cut into pieces
3	cups cubed cooked turkey or chicken
1	package (10 ounces) frozen French cut green beans, thawed
1	can (11 ounces) condensed cheddar cheese soup
¾	cup milk

MIX contents of vegetable/seasoning packet, hot water and butter in large bowl until butter is melted. Stir in stuffing crumbs just to moisten. Let stand 5 minutes.

MIX turkey and green beans in 2-quart casserole or 12x8-inch baking dish. Mix soup and milk in medium bowl until smooth; pour over turkey mixture. Spoon stuffing evenly over top.

BAKE at 350°F for 30 minutes or until thoroughly heated.

Makes 6 servings.

VARIATION: Substitute 3 cups STOVE TOP Chicken Flavor Stuffing Mix in the Canister for Savory Herb Stuffing Mix. Decrease water to 1¼ cups and butter to 3 tablespoons.

From left: Easy Classic Lasagna (recipe, page 74)
Turkey and Green Bean Casserole

EASY CLASSIC LASAGNA

*When sharing this popular dish with neighbors and friends,
don't forget to share the recipe, too (photo, page 72).*

Prep time: 20 minutes
Baking time: 30 minutes plus standing

- 1 pound ground beef
- ½ cup chopped onion
- 1 jar (28 ounces) spaghetti sauce
- 9 lasagna noodles, cooked, drained
- 1 container (16 ounces) BREAKSTONE'S *or* KNUDSEN Cottage Cheese
- 3 cups (12 ounces) KRAFT Natural Shredded Low-Moisture Part-Skim Mozzarella Cheese
- ½ cup (2 ounces) KRAFT 100% Grated Parmesan Cheese

BROWN meat in large skillet on medium-high heat; drain. Add onion; cook until tender. Stir in sauce; cover. Reduce heat to low; simmer 15 minutes.

LAYER 3 noodles, ⅓ of the meat sauce, ½ of the cottage cheese and ⅓ of the mozzarella cheese in 13x9-inch baking dish; repeat layers. Top with remaining 3 noodles, meat sauce and mozzarella cheese. Sprinkle with Parmesan cheese.

BAKE at 350°F for 30 minutes. Let stand 10 minutes before serving.

Makes 6 to 8 servings.

BEST OF SPRING

Onions

Onion varieties are numerous, and there are particular specialties according to the season. In the spring and summer, dry bulb onions with a mild, sweet and somewhat less pungent flavor than fall and winter onions appear in the markets. They can be white, yellow or red, and sometimes are referred to as fresh onions. They commonly have thin, papery outer skins and a high water and sugar content, which makes them both sweet and juicy, but also makes them fragile, bruise easily and have a fairly short shelf life.

Each spring, onion-lovers look forward to the arrival of special sweet-onion varieties such as Vidalia, Walla Walla, Maui, Texas Spring Sweet, Imperial Sweet and Carzalia Sweet.

Keep spring and summer onions in the refrigerator for up to several weeks. You'll not only keep them fresh, but also help cut down on the crying when you do cut them—a chilled onion produces fewer tears.

Plan on 1 small onion to make ⅓ cup chopped, 1 medium onion to make ½ cup chopped, 1 large onion to make 1 cup chopped and 1 green onion to make 2 tablespoons sliced.

CHICKEN SOUR CREAM ENCHILADAS

*If you don't have leftover cooked chicken for this
Tex-Mex favorite, use chopped frozen cooked chicken from
the freezer case of your grocery store.*

Prep time: 20 minutes
Baking time: 35 minutes

- 1 container (16 ounces) BREAKSTONE'S *or* KNUDSEN Sour Cream, divided
- 2 cups chopped cooked chicken
- 1 package (8 ounces) KRAFT Natural *or* ⅓ Less Fat Shredded Reduced Fat Colby and Monterey Jack Cheese, divided
- 1 cup salsa, divided
- 2 tablespoons chopped cilantro
- 1 teaspoon ground cumin
- 10 flour tortillas (6 inches)
- 1 cup shredded lettuce
- ½ cup chopped tomato

MIX 1 cup of the sour cream, chicken, 1 cup of the cheese, ¼ cup of the salsa, cilantro and cumin.

SPOON about ¼ cup of the chicken mixture down center of each tortilla; roll up. Place, seam-side down, in 13x9-inch baking dish. Top with remaining ¾ cup salsa; cover.

BAKE at 350°F for 30 minutes. Sprinkle with remaining 1 cup cheese. Bake an additional 5 minutes or until cheese is melted. Top with lettuce and tomato. Serve with remaining 1 cup sour cream.

Makes 5 servings.

TRADITIONAL EASTER DINNER

Here's a crowd-pleasing meal for this joyous holiday.

Delicious Deviled Eggs

Baked ham*

VELVEETA® Cheese Spread Cheesy Rice & Broccoli

Mixed salad greens with desired **KRAFT** pourable
dressing

Honey Raisin Bread

Sour Cream Pound Cake with fresh berries *or*

COOL 'N EASY™ Easter Pie

MAXWELL HOUSE
Rich French Roast Coffee

*Prepare your favorite recipe.

SOUR CREAM POUND CAKE

*For a seasonal touch, top with COOL WHIP Whipped Topping
and strawberries (photo, left and on the cover).*

Prep time: 25 minutes
Baking time: 1 hour and 15 minutes plus cooling

　3　cups flour
　½　teaspoon baking soda
　1　cup (2 sticks) butter *or* margarine
　2¼　cups granulated sugar
　1　teaspoon vanilla
　6　eggs
　1　cup BREAKSTONE'S *or* KNUDSEN Sour Cream
　　　Powdered sugar

MIX flour and baking soda in medium bowl. Beat
butter in large bowl with electric mixer on
medium speed until softened. Gradually add
granulated sugar, beating until light and fluffy.
Blend in vanilla. Add eggs, 1 at a time, mixing
well after each addition. Add flour mixture
alternately with sour cream, mixing well after
each addition.

SPOON into greased and floured 12-cup fluted
tube pan or 10-inch tube pan.

BAKE in preheated 325°F oven for 1 hour and
10 minutes to 1 hour and 15 minutes or until
toothpick inserted in center comes out clean. Cool
10 minutes in pan on wire rack; remove from pan.
Cool completely on wire rack. Sprinkle with
powdered sugar.

Makes 16 servings.

Sour Cream Pound Cake
COOL 'N EASY™ *Easter Pie (recipe, page 79)*

DELICIOUS DEVILED EGGS

For a first-rate presentation, pipe the yolk mixture into the egg-white cavities using decorating bag with a large star tip.

Prep time: 30 minutes plus refrigerating

- 12 hard-cooked eggs
- ½ cup KRAFT Real Mayonnaise
- 2 teaspoons finely grated onion
- 1 teaspoon Dijon mustard
- ⅛ teaspoon *each* ground black pepper, ground red pepper *and* salt
- Paprika (optional)

CUT eggs in half lengthwise. Remove yolks; mash in small bowl.

STIR in mayonnaise, onion, mustard, black pepper, red pepper and salt until smooth.

SPOON or pipe into centers of egg whites. Cover. Refrigerate until ready to serve. Sprinkle with paprika.

Makes 24.

VELVEETA CHEESE SPREAD CHEESY RICE & BROCCOLI

This simple and elegant side dish not only tastes delicious, but adds a spring-green touch to the Easter table, too.

Prep time: 5 minutes
Cooking time: 10 minutes plus standing

- 1 package (16 ounces) frozen broccoli cuts
- 1½ cups water
- 1 pound (16 ounces) VELVEETA Pasteurized Process Cheese Spread *or* VELVEETA LIGHT Pasteurized Process Cheese Product, cut up
- 3 cups MINUTE Original Rice, uncooked

BRING broccoli and water to full boil in medium saucepan on medium-high heat, separating broccoli with fork.

STIR in process cheese spread. Reduce heat to low; cover and simmer 4 minutes.

STIR in rice; cover. Remove from heat and let stand 5 minutes. Stir before serving.

Makes 12 servings.

HONEY RAISIN BREAD

For a festive look, serve this quick bread with whipped butter piped into a lemon shell and decorated with a fresh herb leaf.

Prep time: 15 minutes
Baking time: 60 minutes plus cooling

1¾ cups flour

2½ teaspoons CALUMET Baking Powder

½ teaspoon salt

⅔ cup POST GRAPE-NUTS Cereal

1 cup milk

1 egg, slightly beaten

⅔ cup firmly packed brown sugar

¼ cup honey

3 tablespoons butter *or* margarine, melted

⅔ cup raisins *or* dried apricots, finely chopped

MIX flour, baking powder and salt in large bowl. Mix cereal and milk in another bowl; let stand 5 minutes. Stir in egg, sugar, honey and butter. Add to flour mixture; stir just until moistened. (Batter will be lumpy.) Stir in raisins.

POUR into 8x4-inch loaf pan that has been sprayed with no stick cooking spray.

BAKE in preheated 350°F oven for 50 minutes or until toothpick inserted in center comes out clean. Cool 10 minutes; remove from pan. Cool completely on wire rack.

Makes 1 loaf.

Note: For easier slicing, wrap bread and store overnight.

COOL 'N EASY™ EASTER PIE

This pretty pie will brighten your holiday table (photo, page 76).

Prep time: 20 minutes plus refrigerating

⅔ cup boiling water

1 package (4-serving size) JELL-O Brand Strawberry Flavor Gelatin Dessert *or* any red flavor

½ cup cold water

Ice cubes

1 tub (12 ounces) COOL WHIP Whipped Topping, thawed

1 cup chopped strawberries

1 prepared graham cracker crumb crust (6 ounces *or* 9 inches)

STIR boiling water into gelatin in large bowl 2 minutes or until completely dissolved. Mix cold water and ice cubes to make 1¼ cups. Add to gelatin, stirring until slightly thickened. Remove any remaining ice.

STIR in 3½ cups of the whipped topping with wire whisk until smooth. Mix in strawberries. Refrigerate 20 to 30 minutes or until mixture is very thick and will mound. Spoon into crust.

REFRIGERATE 4 hours or until firm. Garnish with remaining whipped topping and additional strawberries, if desired. Store leftover pie in refrigerator.

Makes 8 servings.

Dad's Birthday Party

Get the whole family involved in Dad's special meal. The kids can help prepare and garnish the pie while Mom makes the rest of the dinner.

Peach-Glazed Pork Chops

Roasted Italian Potatoes

Steamed sugarsnap peas*

Rocky Road Chocolate Silk Pie

GENERAL FOODS INTERNATIONAL COFFEES
Italian Cappuccino *or* Suisse Mocha Flavor

*Prepare your favorite recipe.

Rocky Road Chocolate Silk Pie

There's nothing rocky about the road to making this melt-in-your-mouth pie—it's smooth sailing, thanks to JELL-O No Bake Chocolate Silk Pie mix.

Prep time: 20 minutes plus refrigerating

- 1 package (9.2 ounces) JELL-O Brand No Bake Chocolate Silk Pie
- ⅓ cup butter *or* margarine, melted
- 1⅔ cups cold milk
- 1 cup miniature marshmallows
- ½ cup chopped nuts

MIX crumbs and butter thoroughly with fork in 9-inch pie plate until crumbs are well moistened. Press firmly against sides of pie plate first, using finger or large spoon to shape edge. Press remaining crumbs firmly onto bottom using measuring cup.

BEAT cold milk and filling mix with electric mixer on low speed until blended. Beat on medium speed 3 minutes. (Filling will be thick.) Stir in marshmallows and nuts. Spoon into crust.

REFRIGERATE at least 1 hour. Garnish with thawed COOL WHIP Whipped Topping and decorative candy sprinkles, if desired. Store leftover pie in refrigerator.

Makes 8 servings.

Rocky Road Chocolate Silk Pie

PEACH-GLAZED PORK CHOPS

This pork-chop dish comes wrapped in a pretty, peachy glaze that goes together simply, so you can save time for unwrapping presents.

Prep time: 15 minutes
Baking time: 40 minutes

- 1 can (8½ ounces) peach slices, undrained
  Hot water
- 1 package (6 ounces) STOVE TOP Stuffing Mix for Pork
- ¼ cup (½ stick) butter *or* margarine, cut into pieces
- 6 pork chops, ½ inch thick
- ⅓ cup peach *or* apricot preserves
- 1 tablespoon Dijon mustard

DRAIN peaches, reserving syrup. Add hot water to syrup to measure 1½ cups. Mix syrup mixture, contents of vegetable/seasoning packet and butter in large bowl until butter is melted. Stir in stuffing crumbs and peaches. Let stand 5 minutes.

SPOON stuffing into 13x9-inch baking pan. Arrange chops over stuffing. Mix preserves and mustard. Spoon over chops.

BAKE at 375°F for 40 minutes or until chops are cooked through.

Makes 6 servings.

ROASTED ITALIAN POTATOES

These zesty herbed potatoes tossed with Parmesan cheese are a perfect foil for the sweetness of the Peach-Glazed Pork Chops.

Prep time: 10 minutes
Baking time: 45 minutes

- 2 pounds potatoes, cut into quarters
- ½ cup KRAFT Zesty Italian Dressing
- ½ cup (2 ounces) KRAFT 100% Grated Parmesan Cheese

TOSS potatoes with dressing and cheese. Place in 13x9-inch baking pan.

BAKE at 400°F for 40 to 45 minutes or until lightly browned.

Makes 6 to 8 servings.

Roasted Italian Potatoes
Peach-Glazed Pork Chops

COME FOR LUNCH

This meatless meal is a refreshing way to feast with family and friends after a bike ride, golf game or long walk in the park.

Italian Vegetable Dip with assorted crudités

Cheesy Vegetable Grills

Fresh fruit kabobs
(papaya, strawberries and kiwi)

Raspberry Coconut Bars

Sparkling water *or*

GENERAL FOODS INTERNATIONAL COFFEES
French Vanilla Cafe Flavor

CHEESY VEGETABLE GRILLS

Grilled cheese sandwiches get a makeover when they're filled with tomatoes, sweet peppers and onion slices.

Prep time: 5 minutes
Cooking time: 10 minutes

- 8 slices whole grain bread
- 4 teaspoons Dijon mustard
- ¼ pound (4 ounces) VELVEETA Pasteurized Process Cheese Spread, sliced
- 1 green pepper, cut into rings
- 4 thin onion slices
- 4 slices tomato
- 8 teaspoons butter *or* margarine, softened

SPREAD 1 side of 4 bread slices each with 1 teaspoon mustard. Top with process cheese spread, green pepper, onion, tomato and second bread slice.

SPREAD sandwiches with 1 teaspoon butter on each outer side. Cook in large skillet on medium heat until lightly browned on both sides.

Makes 4 sandwiches.

Raspberry Coconut Bars (recipe, page 87)
Cheesy Vegetable Grills

ITALIAN VEGETABLE DIP

This easy sour cream dip is boldly flavored with
GOOD SEASONS Zesty Italian Salad Dressing Mix. Serve it
with your favorite medley of munchies.

Prep time: 10 minutes plus refrigerating

1 cup BREAKSTONE'S *or* KNUDSEN Sour Cream

1 cup KRAFT Real Mayonnaise

1 envelope GOOD SEASONS Zesty Italian Salad
    Dressing Mix

¼ cup *each* finely chopped green *and*
    red pepper

MIX sour cream, mayonnaise and salad
dressing mix.

STIR in green and red pepper. Refrigerate.

SERVE with assorted cut-up vegetables, boiled
potatoes, breadsticks or chips.

Makes 2¼ cups.

BEST OF SPRING

Great Garnishes from the Garden

Add a splash of color and a touch of elegance to your springtime desserts, salads, entrées and appetizers with a beautiful floral garnish. Whether you use whole blossoms or a scattering of petals, be sure the flowers are a nontoxic variety and free of any chemicals. (Flowers from a florist usually are treated with chemicals and should not be used.) Favorite flowers for food use include the rose, viola, pansy, calendula (pot marigold), daylily, nasturtium, violet, chamomile, bachelor's button, carnation, geranium blossom (not leaf) and magnolia. If you have any doubt about whether a flower's blossom, stem or leaf is edible, check with your local poison control center or state extension service. You can use unsprayed edible flowers from your own garden. Or obtain flowers from the produce section of some supermarkets or from a restaurant or produce supplier who specializes in edible flowers.

RASPBERRY COCONUT BARS

*BAKER'S ANGEL FLAKE Coconut adds a heavenly touch to these
colorful fruit bars (photo, page 84).*

Prep time: 15 minutes
Baking time: 45 minutes plus cooling

1¼ cups flour
¼ teaspoon salt
½ cup (1 stick) butter *or* margarine, cut into chunks
3 tablespoons cold water
2 eggs
½ cup sugar
2⅔ cups (7 ounces) BAKER'S ANGEL FLAKE Coconut
⅓ cup KRAFT Red Raspberry Preserves

MIX flour and salt in medium bowl. Cut in butter until coarse crumbs form. Sprinkle water over mixture while tossing to blend well. Press evenly onto bottom of ungreased 9-inch square pan.

BAKE in preheated 425°F oven for 20 minutes or until lightly browned. Decrease oven temperature to 350°F.

BEAT eggs in large bowl with electric mixer on high speed. Gradually add sugar, beating until thick and light in color. Gently stir in coconut. Spread preserves over crust to within ¼ inch of edges. Carefully spread coconut mixture over preserves.

BAKE 25 minutes or until golden brown. Cool completely on wire rack. Cut into bars.

Makes 2 dozen.

Glistening Candied Flowers

What's the secret to the stunning look of the glistening flowers on the **PHILLY** Cream Cheese Classic Cheesecake shown on the cover and page 63? They're candied edible flowers, which you easily can prepare at home. Gently wash fresh edible flowers (see information, opposite) in water, then place them on white paper towels to air dry. Using a small, clean paintbrush, brush the petals with a mixture of 1 tablespoon meringue powder and 2 tablespoons water. (Look for meringue powder in specialty shops or craft stores with cake-decorating supplies.) Sprinkle the flowers with extra-fine-grain sugar, then shake off excess and let the flowers dry on wax paper for 2 to 4 hours.

If you like, you can store candied flowers in an airtight container between layers of wax paper for up to 1 week. For longer storage, freeze them for up to 6 months.

DRESSING YOUR TABLE

Setting the table is
more than simply arranging the
dishes: It's staging the scene.
A thoughtfully dressed table
complements the food and
enhances the mood. Yet it
doesn't have to be complicated.
This chapter covers the basics
and touches on some innovative
ideas for adding your own
flourish to the occasion.
You'll find that dressing a table
is not only an essential part of
entertaining—it's also
part of the fun!

BEGINNINGS

When planning how to dress your table, it's helpful to think about how you yourself will dress. While your best pearls might call for formal china, a lace tablecloth and a centerpiece of roses, sneakers and jeans may warrant a cotton red-and-white checkered cloth, pottery plates and pots of fresh-cut daisies. Whether casual or fancy or anywhere in between, the linens, centerpiece and tableware you choose can bring a bit of your own personal flair to the table.

TABLE COVERINGS

The tablecloth is the stage on which your food drama will unfold. While there are many styles of brightly colored and printed cotton cloths that work well for casual occasions, you can't go wrong with a simple neutral tablecloth for both casual and formal uses. It lends a clean, fresh look to your table, putting your dishes in their best possible light. When choosing fabrics, cotton tablecloths are best for casual events, while linen and lace tablecloths work well for formal affairs (photo, right).

When you want to add a splash of color and texture to your neutral cloth, consider using a table runner and place mats of straw, cotton or linen. This will also provide protection against spills.

For a creative touch, use an old quilt or quilt fragment as a tablecloth (photo, right). Again, you may wish to use place mats to keep it clean. To add romance, try a layer or two of antique white lace over your linens. A colored tablecloth placed under the lace will accent the distinctively patterned cutouts.

CENTERPIECES

A well-chosen centerpiece is the crowning glory of the table, communicating the season or symbolizing the event being celebrated. For this time of year, try a pot of hyacinths for a spring luncheon, blooming lilies for an Easter dinner or a pitcher of lilacs for a baby or wedding shower buffet.

To fashion a floral centerpiece, match the flowers to the mood of the occasion. Some flowers, such as white roses, feel more formal; others, like black-eyed Susans or brightly colored phlox, can bring an informal, spirited touch to the table.

Try varying the vessel for your centerpiece bouquets: While roses in a crystal vase seem formal, those same roses in an antique watering can may offer the easygoing look you're seeking. Or, gather a collection of small whimsical glass bottles, vases or tiny jars that can hold one or two flowers each, then cluster the arrangement in the center of the table.

Be sure your centerpiece is not so tall that it obscures one guest from another, or could be knocked over as food is passed. On the other hand, taller flowers work well at buffet tables, since guests most likely will be standing when serving themselves. Also the flowers you choose should not be strong smelling, as their fragrance can interfere with the appetizing aromas of the food.

When fresh flowers are scarce, a year-round option is a bowl of artfully arranged fresh fruits. The fruits you choose should complement the season as well. Oranges and apples are appropriate in winter, while strawberries and plums suit the spring (photo, below).

Tableware

Just as a pure white or neutral tablecloth is a quintessential foundation for a table, pure white or neutral dinnerware provides a classic carriage for your food. The colors of almost all foods present themselves beautifully on white dishes—whether they're of china or bone china for a formal affair or earthenware, ironstone or porcelain for a casual get-together.

While white dishes offer versatility, patterned or solid-color dinnerware lend punch and panache to a table. You may even want to mix and match. There are no rules against mixing floral china with contemporary solid-color china or antique floral pottery with brightly colored pottery. For an impressive effect, you may want to match the flowers in your centerpiece with the flowers on your china.

When selecting tableware, you can include many accessories, such as a bone plate and gravy boat, but the staples are these: dinner plate, salad/dessert plate, coffee cup and saucer, water glass, wineglass (if serving wine), salad/dessert fork, dinner fork, dinner knife, soup spoon (if serving soup) and teaspoon.

PLAIN AND FANCY NAPKINS

There are many kinds of napkins, but the basics are easy to grasp: Dinner napkins are larger than luncheon napkins, and linen napkins are dressier than cotton ones. Just be sure that the fabric colors and texture of your napkins match your tablecloth, runner or place mats. For a crisp-looking table, simply fold napkins into squares or rectangles and press them.

For an exquisite effect, follow the diagrams below for creating these fancy folds:

BUFFET STYLE

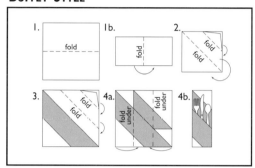

1. *Start with a flat, uncreased, 16-inch napkin. Fold the napkin in half twice. Turn napkin so loose corners are on the top and right sides.* **2.** *Fold down the top right-hand corner 3 inches. Fold down another 2½ inches.* **3.** *Fold down the second right-hand corner 2½ inches. Tuck the second flap under the first.* **4.** *Fold the left and right sides to the back. If desired, insert flatware.*

LILIES

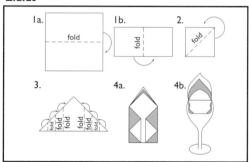

1. *Start with a flat, uncreased napkin. Fold the napkin in half twice.* **2.** *Fold the napkin in half again, forming a triangle.* **3.** *Turn the napkin so the base of the triangle is facing you. Pleat to the center in 1-inch intervals from both the left and right points.* **4.** *Set base in a wineglass. Unfold top points so they fall softly toward the front of the glass.*

BABY BUNTING

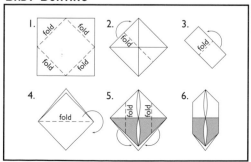

1. *Start with a flat, uncreased napkin. Fold the four corners to the center.* **2.** *Fold in half by bringing the bottom edge up to the top edge.* **3.** *Fold in half again by bringing the right side over to the left side.* **4.** *Turn so the loose points are at the top. Take the first top point and fold it down so it is 1 inch from the bottom point.* **5.** *Fold the right and left points to the back so they overlap. Lay flat.*

INDEX

BEST OF SPRING

Cooking Hints for Metric Users

By making a few conversions, cooks in Australia, Canada, and the United Kingdom can use the recipes in *Springtime Celebrations* with confidence. The charts on this page provide a guide for converting measurements from the U.S. customary system, which is used throughout this book, to the imperial and metric systems. There also is a conversion table for oven temperatures to accommodate the differences in oven calibrations.

Product Differences: Most of the ingredients called for in the recipes in this book are available in English-speaking countries. However, some are known by different names. Here are some common American ingredients and their possible counterparts:
■ Sugar is granulated or castor sugar.
■ Powdered sugar is icing sugar.
■ All-purpose flour is plain household flour or white flour. When self-rising flour is used in place of all-purpose flour in a recipe that calls for leavening, omit the leavening agent (baking soda or baking powder) and salt.
■ Light corn syrup is golden syrup.
■ Cornstarch is cornflour.
■ Baking soda is bicarbonate of soda.
■ Vanilla is vanilla essence.
■ Green, red, or yellow sweet peppers are capsicums.
■ Golden raisins are sultanas.

Volume and Weight: Americans traditionally use cup measures for liquid and solid ingredients. The chart, *top right,* shows the approximate imperial and metric equivalents. If you are accustomed to weighing solid ingredients, the following approximate equivalents will be helpful.
■ 1 cup butter, castor sugar, or rice = 8 ounces = about 250 grams
■ 1 cup flour = 4 ounces = about 125 grams
■ 1 cup icing sugar = 5 ounces = about 150 grams

Spoon measures are used for smaller amounts of ingredients. Although the size of the tablespoon varies slightly in different countries, for practical purposes and for recipes in this book, a straight substitution is all that's necessary.

Measurements made using cups or spoons always should be level unless stated otherwise.

Equivalents: U.S. = Australia/U.K.

⅛ teaspoon = 0.5 ml
¼ teaspoon = 1 ml
½ teaspoon = 2 ml
1 teaspoon = 5 ml
1 tablespoon = 1 tablespoon
¼ cup = 2 tablespoons = 2 fluid ounces = 60 ml
⅓ cup = ¼ cup = 3 fluid ounces = 90 ml
½ cup = ⅓ cup = 4 fluid ounces = 120 ml

⅔ cup = ½ cup = 5 fluid ounces = 150 ml
¾ cup = ⅔ cup = 6 fluid ounces = 180 ml
1 cup = ¾ cup = 8 fluid ounces = 240 ml
1¼ cups = 1 cup
2 cups = 1 pint
1 quart = 1 litre
½ inch = 1.27 cm
1 inch = 2.54 cm

Baking Pan Sizes

American	Metric
8x1½-inch round	20x4-centimetre cake tin baking pan
9x1½-inch round	23x3.5-centimetre cake tin baking pan
11x7x1½-inch baking pan	28x18x4-centimetre baking tin
13x9x2-inch baking pan	30x20x3-centimetre baking tin
2-quart rectangular baking dish	30x20x3-centimetre baking tin
15½x10½x2-inch baking pan	30x25x2-centimetre baking tin (Swiss roll tin)
9-inch pie plate	22x4- or 23x4-centimetre pie plate
7- or 8-inch springform pan	18- or 20-centimetre springform or loose-bottom cake tin
9x5x3-inch loaf pan	23x13x7-centimetre or 2-pound narrow loaf tin or paté tin
1½-quart casserole	1.5-litre casserole
2-quart casserole	2-litre casserole

Oven Temperature Equivalents

Fahrenheit Setting	Celsius Setting*	Gas Setting
300°F	150°C	Gas Mark 2 (slow)
325°F	160°C	Gas Mark 3 (moderately slow)
350°F	180°C	Gas Mark 4 (moderate)
375°F	190°C	Gas Mark 5 (moderately hot)
400°F	200°C	Gas Mark 6 (hot)
425°F	220°C	Gas Mark 7
450°F	230°C	Gas Mark 8 (very hot)
Broil		Grill

Electric and gas ovens may be calibrated using Celsius. However, for an electric oven, increase the Celsius setting 10° to 20° when cooking above 160°C. For convection or forced-air ovens (gas or electric), lower the temperature setting 10°C when cooking at all heat levels.